THE LONG JOURNEY HOME
Parables and Wisdom from the Little Prince

ROBERT R. FUGGI

Copyright © 2024 Robert R. Fuggi.

All rights reserved. No part of this book may be used or reproduced by any means, graphic, electronic, or mechanical, including photocopying, recording, taping or by any information storage retrieval system without the written permission of the author except in the case of brief quotations embodied in critical articles and reviews.

WestBow Press books may be ordered through booksellers or by contacting:

WestBow Press
A Division of Thomas Nelson & Zondervan
1663 Liberty Drive
Bloomington, IN 47403
www.westbowpress.com
844-714-3454

Because of the dynamic nature of the Internet, any web addresses or links contained in this book may have changed since publication and may no longer be valid. The views expressed in this work are solely those of the author and do not necessarily reflect the views of the publisher, and the publisher hereby disclaims any responsibility for them.

Any people depicted in stock imagery provided by Getty Images are models, and such images are being used for illustrative purposes only.
Certain stock imagery © Getty Images.

ISBN: 979-8-3850-1583-2 (sc)
ISBN: 979-8-3850-1585-6 (hc)
ISBN: 979-8-3850-1584-9 (e)

Library of Congress Control Number: 2023924664

Print information available on the last page.

WestBow Press rev. date: 3/7/2024

*For Christian,
my little prince,
and to his rose
and his fox*

*It is only with the heart that one can see rightly;
what is essential is invisible to the eye.*

*If I try to describe him here,
it is to make sure that I shall not forget him.*

Antoine de Saint-Exupéry

Contents

Preface: A Message from the Pilot xi

Chapter 1   We Must Become Like Little Children Again 1
Chapter 2   Draw Me a Sheep 5
Chapter 3   We Entertain Angels 10
Chapter 4   Outward Appearances 13
Chapter 5   A Bad Tree 17
Chapter 6   A Sad Life 20
Chapter 7   One Flower Unique in All the World 23
Chapter 8   Vanity of Vanities 27
Chapter 9   Forgiveness 30
Chapter 10 The King 34
Chapter 11 Clap Your Hands for Me 38
Chapter 12 The Tippler 42
Chapter 13 The Poor Rich Businessman 46
Chapter 14 The Lamplighter 50
Chapter 15 A Good-for-Nothing Geographer 53
Chapter 16 The Earth 56
Chapter 17 The Snake 58
Chapter 18 One Flower, Three Petals 61
Chapter 19 All Alone 65
Chapter 20 The Beloved 67

Chapter 21 The Fox	70
Chapter 22 The Switchman	77
Chapter 23 The Merchant	80
Chapter 24 The Pilot	82
Chapter 25 The Well	85
Chapter 26 The Snake	87
Chapter 27 Going Home	93
Afterword: Six Years On	97

Preface: A Message from the Pilot

Where do I begin? This little book has been birthed out of joy, blessings, pain, and suffering. Almost six years ago, I was delivering a sermon at our local church when my three children, on their way to see me, were involved in a catastrophic accident, one that would alter our lives forevermore, eventually taking the life of my youngest child.

In all the books I have studied and read in my career as both a lawyer and a theologian, I do not recall a book other than the Bible that has so affected me more than the special book titled *The Little Prince*, written by the French aviator Antoine de Saint-Exupéry in 1943 and published posthumously as *Le Petit Prince*. By striking coincidence, the publication of my book marks the eightieth anniversary of the original publication of *The Little Prince*. I hope it is an appropriate homage.

The Little Prince has been translated into hundreds of languages and has sold over 200 million copies worldwide, which makes it one of the best-selling books in history. But I had never heard of the book until my wife went to an exhibit in New York City at the Morgan Museum and was first exposed to its beauty and majesty. As I read *The Little Prince*, I was deeply moved and affected by what I perceive to be the deep underlying theological messages of life, love, sacrifice, separation, death, and restoration. The book I've written is about how *The Little Prince* not only impacted our lives but was instrumental in bringing forth healing from one of life's most difficult circumstances. I have tried to develop its moral, scriptural, and biblical concepts of life and death, but I do not attempt to suggest to the reader that what

I write—the analysis, concepts proffered, analogies, or application—are what Antoine de Saint-Exupéry intended. In fact, I don't know whether he was thinking of any of the things that I propose to write about through a theologian's lens. But I believe the world needs *The Little Prince*'s message of hope and comfort.

I hope my book does no harm to the original masterpiece but rather is a beneficial accompaniment. That is why I might suggest that you read the original book *The Little Prince* first. Think of it as a prerequisite to this book, as English 101 is required before English 102. If you take the time and effort to read *The Little Prince* carefully once, twice, or even three times to fully understand its depth and beauty, then you may be able to see more clearly the theological and spiritual perspectives I have wanted to bring to it. And if you haven't read *The Little Prince*, I hope this book will prompt you to do so.

If you have ever dealt with loss, and most of us have or will, I believe you will find the theological and scriptural insights I found in *The Little Prince* to bring forth hope, love, and most of all comfort. Initially, this book was not intended for anyone other than myself. If more than one person reads and is comforted by it, then the book will have surpassed my expectations.

Chapter 1

We Must Become Like Little Children Again

They were bringing children to him that he might touch them, and the disciples rebuked them. But when Jesus saw it, he was indignant for such belongs the kingdom of God. Truly I say to you whoever does not receive the kingdom of God like a child shall not enter it. And he took them in his arms and blessed them, laying his hands on them.
Mark 10:13–16 (ESV)

In today's digital age, we are overloaded by the information highway, the internet, and have lost much of the simplicity and beauty of life. Have we lost our imagination too? How can we recapture the imagination and innocence of a child?

The first chapter of *The Little Prince* focuses on the imagination and attitude of a child. An adult who has an attitude of a child might be viewed negatively in our society, but I believe that as grown-ups we need to have childlike attributes and characteristics. Life is difficult and filled with uncertainty and loss, and ultimately we will all face death, of loved ones and of ourselves. The question is, how shall we live?

The Little Prince, a children's book written for adults, addresses these important concepts of life and death in a masterful way. We are confronted in the early portions of *The Little Prince* with the pilot as a young child and his first interactions with the adult world. Evidently, he loved to draw, and his first masterpiece was his first drawing: a boa constrictor that swallowed a whole animal. Excited when he completed the drawing, and understanding what the drawing represented, he made the mistake of showing it to his parents and other grown-ups. They thought it was silly and told him it looked like an ordinary hat. They could not use imagination to see the drawing as it was through the imagination of a child.

The grown-ups quickly rejected the notion that this drawing was relevant or important to the young artist. They dismissed the boy and the drawing and told him to use his time wisely in better pursuits. The little boy—the pilot, as we will come to know him—wanted to be an artist, but that dream was quickly dashed. He would never draw again … until he met a curious character called the little prince.

When we encounter this creature of the little prince, the ways we think and live are immediately challenged. As adults, we are told to put away childish things and childish thinking, but is that always the most beneficial? In the life of Christ, we see a time when Jesus was very interested in the children and suggested to adults that they need to become more like children again to better understand the kingdom of God.

During the life of Jesus, a man recognized as from God,[1] people began bringing their little children to Jesus to have him touch them. We don't know whether the children were sick or infirm, or whether the parents just wanted Jesus to touch them as people in today's time want to touch someone of spiritual status or importance, such as the pope. Do people feel that if they could touch the spiritual person, then some special dispensation would occur?

Similarly, in the life of Jesus, there was a woman with a serious

---

[1] The statement "a man recognized as from God" is a moral low Christological understanding of the person and work of Jesus Christ. Describing Jesus as a person who does God's will, performs miracles, or is sent by God would be recognized as a middle Christological understanding. Only the full recognition and understanding that Jesus Christ is in fact God would be a high Christological understanding.

blood disorder who had been subjected to bleeding for twelve years and endured a great deal of pain and suffering. She spent all her money trying to get cured. She knew that if she could only touch Jesus, he would heal her. So she pressed through the crowd that was following Jesus, and she was able to touch his cloak: "She thought, 'If I just touch his clothes, I will be healed.' "[2] As soon as she touched Jesus's clothes, she was immediately healed and freed from her suffering. When this happened, Jesus "realized power had gone out of him ... and asked 'Who touched my clothes?' " When Jesus was finally approached by the woman who was healed, he said to her, "Your faith has made you well; go in peace and be free from your suffering."[3]

Is this a type of childlike faith that we need in our lives today? Life has become so complicated, and people focus on matters that are unimportant until tragedy forces them to reevaluate their priorities in life. The pilot felt much the same way; to him his drawings represented all that was important in life: imagination, dreams, and freedom. When the pilot, as a young boy, tried to share these aspirations with grown-ups, they had no place or time for it.

The disciples reacted much the same way the grown-ups reacted to the pilot. They came to Jesus and asked him, "Who is the greatest in the kingdom of heaven?"[4] In response, Jesus called a little child and said to the disciples, "Unless you change and become like little children, you will never enter the kingdom of heaven."[5] Jesus concluded with the directive "that whoever humbles himself like this child is the greatest in the kingdom of heaven."[6]

Why would Jesus say something so dramatic and contrary to society and cultural values? How could a little child hold the secrets of the kingdom of God? Could it be the childlike faith they possess, or their innocence and love contrary to the evil and hatred present in

---

[2] Mark 5:28 NIV.
[3] Mark 5:30–34 NIV.
[4] Matthew 18:1 NIV.
[5] Matthew 18:3 NIV.
[6] Mark 18:4 NIV.

and of the world? They possess a simplicity and innocence before it is eroded by what we call life.

Could the little prince hold these same virtues? Who is the little prince? Is it the pilot's inner child? We don't know, but *The Little Prince* and its tenants will enable hardened adults who have lost their place in the world, who have seemingly forgot what it is to be a child, to recapture that love and innocence that had been lost.

Scripture suggests that we "as dearly beloved children" live a life of love "just as Christ loved us and gave himself up for us as a fragrant offering."[7] By thinking like the little prince, we, too, may be able to see what drawing number one really represented—a boa constrictor that swallowed a whole animal—and not see it as just a hat.

---

[7] Ephesians 5:1–2 NIV.

Chapter 2

Draw Me a Sheep

I am the good shepherd; I know my sheep and my sheep know me.
John 10:14 (NIV)

The story of the little prince begins when the pilot crashes in the Sahara desert during a test flight on a new plane. Where he has crashed is far from any people, help, or civilization. He quickly realizes that in order to survive, he must be able to repair his plane and get it to fly, or he will be lost. The circumstances are dire.

The pilot is all alone when he encounters for the first time this small creature called the little prince. The pilot cannot understand how and why this seemingly little child could be in the middle of the Sahara desert. Maybe, the pilot thinks, he is starting to hallucinate from the crash, or maybe he hit his head or lacking water and starting to dehydrate. Is this creature real? Or at least is real to him? This is where the whole encounter begins.

The little prince asks the pilot to draw him a sheep, of all things. The pilot is brought immediately back to his childhood, when he loved to draw and hoped someday to be an artist. But as you already know, those dreams were quickly dashed by the grown-ups. Well, here in the Sahara desert, there are no grown-ups, and no one to tell the pilot he cannot or should not draw—except himself. The pilot made his last drawings when he was six years old. Drawing number one depicted a boa constrictor that swallowed an animal whole, and drawing number two depicted the animal that was swallowed whole by the boa constrictor—an elephant.

Now, as the pilot meets the little prince, he is asked to draw a sheep. The pilot thinks, *What an usual request!* The pilot does not want to oblige the little prince in light of his dire circumstances. He does not think he can draw a sheep because, as he puts it, he stopped drawing at a young age and was never able to draw anything other than the boa constrictor that swallowed an animal whole, which grown-ups thought looked like a hat.

The pilot has difficulty understanding this encounter with the little prince. The pilot's situation is dire; without water, supplies, food, and the proper equipment to repair his airplane, he is contemplating a serious and unpleasant outcome. In the middle of this circumstance, the pilot has to oblige this little creature in his request to draw a sheep. Of all the animals the little prince could have requested the pilot to draw—a lion, a tiger, a bear, an eagle, a whale—the child requests a sheep. Why a sheep, you may ask? Does the selection of a sheep have any theological significance?

Sheep are mentioned throughout the Bible in both the Old and the New Testaments, but what do sheep signify biblically?

> Sheep are significant throughout the Bible. We can learn a lot about God and his dealings with humanity by understanding their nature. They teach us about ourselves and our helplessness without Christ.[8]

Importantly, Jesus compares the people of his time to sheep: "When he saw the crowds, he had compassion on them, because they were harassed and helpless, like sheep without a shepherd."[9]

Does the little prince want a sheep so he can care, love, and protect it as a real shepherd would? Does the sheep have any theological or

---

[8] "What is the Significance of Sheep in the Bible?" Got Questions, accessed November 27, 2023, www.gotquestions.org/sheep-in-the-Bible.html.
[9] Matthew 9:36 NIV.

spiritual meaning in *The Little Prince*? These are the items we shall discuss further.

Jesus taught a parable about sheep in the Gospel of Luke:

> Suppose one of you has a hundred sheep and lost one of them. Does he not leave the ninety-nine in the open country and go after the lost sheep until he finds it? And when he finds it, he joyfully puts it on his shoulders and goes home. Then he calls his friends and neighbors together and says, "Rejoice with me; I have found my lost sheep."[10]

This parable stands for the spiritual concept of the importance of one person who has been found by their Savior Jesus Christ the great shepherd.

Each individual is important to God. We all are like sheep lost and unable to protect ourselves in the world we live in. I do not mean that in a physical or forceful way, because we see the terrible violence and hatred in the world, but rather spiritually. We are all in a way like the one lost sheep that God searches for and pursues until he finds it. The Old Testament book of Isaiah contemplates a similar message: "He shall feed his flock like a shepherd: He shall gather his lambs with His arms, and carry them to His bosom and shall gently lead those that are with young."[11]

This is a beautiful picture of a shepherd, but the most powerful image of a lamb/sheep may be found in the book of Revelation, in a vivid picture imagining the Lamb at the judgment of the world:

> And when he had taken the book, the four beasts and four and twenty elders fell down before the Lamb … saying with a loud voice, Worthy is the Lamb that

---

[10] Luke 15:4–6 NIV.
[11] Isaiah 40:11 KJV.

was slain to receive power, and riches, and wisdom, and strength, and honour, and glory, and blessing.[12]

Is the lamb or sheep a picture or representation of Jesus Christ and his sacrifice for all humans, as the lamb that was slain for our sins? Could that be why the little prince was so persistent in asking the pilot to draw a proper sheep? Not one too big, or one with horns, nor one too old or sickly, but his sheep must be just right!

Interestingly, one of the final directives Jesus gave before his crucifixion was a reference to lambs and sheep—a lamb without blemish or defect, much like the sheep the little prince requests. First Peter 1:19–21 (NIV) states that we are redeemed

> with the precious blood of Christ, a lamb without blemish or defect. He was chosen before the creation of the world, but was revealed in these last times for your sake. Through him you believe in God, who raised him from the dead and glorified him, and so your faith and hope are in God.

Could Saint-Exupéry be referencing a great Christological concept when the little prince says, "Draw me a sheep"?

In the Gospel of John, Jesus asks Peter, "Do you love me more than the other disciples?" What an odd question for Jesus to ask Peter! Just a few days before the Last Supper, the apostles had been arguing amongst themselves as to who was the greatest of them all. Now Jesus reverses the question and asks Peter directly, "Do you love me more than the others?" Peter answers, "Yes, you know I do, Lord." Then Jesus tells Peter to feed his lambs. Jesus asks Peter a second time, "Do you love me more than the others?" Peter again answers yes, and Jesus again says to Peter, "Feed my sheep." Jesus asks the question of Peter a third time. Peter grieves and says, "Lord, you know that I love you." Jesus once again replies, "Feed my sheep."[13]

---

[12] Revelation 5:8, 12 KJV.
[13] John 21:15–17 KJV.

In the Bible, the terms *lamb* and *sheep* are interchangeable and often refer not only to the church but also to Jesus as the sheep or lamb gone to slaughter as a sin offering. The sheep has a deep theological meaning. Was it by coincidence that it was the animal most important to the little prince?

Chapter 3

We Entertain Angels

See that you do not despise one of these little ones. For I tell you that their angels in heaven always see the face of my Father in heaven.
Matthew 18:10 (NIV)

This chapter of *The Little Prince* is somewhat special, odd, and obscure. The only information we have is that the pilot was trying to ask the little prince questions about how he arrived or appeared in the middle of the Sahara desert alone, with no water, supplies, food, and seemingly unconcerned about those necessary creaturely needs. The little prince appeared rather joyful in his responses, or lack of responses, to the pilot's questioning of how he got there and where he was from. The little prince did not address the pilot's questions with a tangible or responsive answer, but only with laughter!

This to a degree irritated the pilot, but it may be that if the little prince had answered the pilot's questions, the pilot would not have believed the answer. I'm reminded of one of the scriptural references: "Do not forget to entertain strangers, for by doing so some people have entertained angels without knowing it."[14] Is this what the little prince is, an angel who has fallen out of the sky to visit, comfort, and heal the pilot?

Many questions remained mysterious to the pilot about this strange

---

[14] Hebrews 13:2 NIV.

little creature. The answers to those questions were unimportant not only to the little prince but also at this point to the pilot, who has just failed to realize it. In life we focus on unimportant and insignificant things until something significant reorders the priorities of our lives. As adults we lose focus on the here and now and worry about the future or things we cannot control or change.

Was the little prince sent to comfort, heal, and restore the pilot through this encounter? God has promised through scripture that "Never will I leave you; never will I forsake you."[15] All these questions that the pilot has of the little prince—asking "Which planet did you come from?" or "My little man, where did you come from, where do you want to take your sheep?"—received terse responses from the little prince: "That doesn't matter."[16] Could the little prince be an angel, an aberration, or a figment of the pilot's imagination or of his own subconscious? We don't know, but whatever he may or not be, he makes the pilot question the important things of life.

When angels are referred to in the Bible, they always have the same objective: to do the will of God who sent them. They may be messengers of God to bring news, like the angels who announced to Mary that she would give birth to a child:

> God sent the angel Gabriel to Nazareth, a town in Galilee to a virgin pledged to be married to a man named Joseph, a descendant of David. The virgin's name was Mary." ... The angel said to her, "Do not be afraid Mary, you have found favor with God. You will be with child and give birth to a son, and you are to give him the name Jesus."[17]

This was an angel sent by God with good news and blessings.

We also see that angels could bring answers to prayers or news of judgment. In Daniel's case, the angel Gabriel came in response to

---

[15] Hebrews 13:5 NIV.
[16] Antoine de Saint-Exupéry, *The Little Prince*, p. 20.
[17] Luke 1:26–27, 8:30–31 NIV.

Daniel's prayer being heard and answered by God: "At the beginning of that supplication the commandment came forth and I am come to show thee that though art greatly beloved."[18] Angels appear in scripture to both deliver blessings and God's judgment to humanity. These spiritual creatures were created and sustained by God to carry out his will in the universe.

Is the little prince an angel sent by God to the pilot? Angels can be considered helpers, messengers, and workmen. Angels can also give a glimpse of what the resurrection or afterlife is. Jesus taught on the subject of heaven and angels. In the Gospel of Luke, Jesus told the people about the afterlife. There is no marriage in the resurrection. People will no longer feel pain, suffer, or be disabled but rather will be like angels and children of the resurrection.[19] They will be whole spiritual beings with no memory of pain, suffering, or loss of the world from which they came. God has always used angels as messengers to deliver important news, comfort, and judgment to individuals. We know angels also come and aid people in times of need. Angels came and ministered to Jesus after his forty days in the desert when he was being tempted by Satan: "Then the devil left him, and angels came and attended him."[20]

The pilot, too, is now in dire need in the desert. Could this be similar to what happened to Jesus? Had God sent a messenger, a little angel in the little prince, to minister to the pilot? Why? The pilot has carried sorrow, rejection, loneliness, and regret since he was a small child. Through this encounter with the little prince, is it possible that forgiveness and restoration may occur in the pilot's life, even though the little creature has failed to answer any of the pilot's questions?

---

[18] Daniel 9:23 KJV.
[19] Luke 20:34–36 NIV.
[20] Matthew 4:11 NIV.

Chapter 4

Outward Appearances

The Lord said unto Samuel "Do not look onto his countenance or the height of his stature, because I have refused him; for the Lord seeth; for man looketh at the outward appearance but the Lord looketh on the heart."
Samuel 16:17 (KJV)

The pilot assumes that he has figured out where the little prince came from. The way in which he arrived at that conclusion appears to be only speculation. The only detail that the little prince told the pilot relating to where he came from was that his planet was very small. Why the pilot assumes that the "planet" had to be asteroid B-612 is somewhat of a mystery. The pilot goes on to tell a story about how asteroid B-612 was discovered by a Turkish astronomer in 1909. Whether that is true or not is of no consequence to the meaning of the story here. The astronomer who discovered asteroid B-612 is said not to have been taken seriously for his discovery because of his odd appearance and dress. Because he dressed in Turkish costume, he was rejected as a serious scientist or astronomer because of his outward appearance.

Did the pilot reject what the little prince had to offer because he dressed in a blue cape with a scarf and appeared as a little child? Eventually the Turkish astronomer received a directive from the ruling dictator that everyone ought to wear European garb. Shortly after this directive, the Turkish astronomer's theory was received. Now the discovery of asteroid B-612 will be accepted as true. It was the opinion of the pilot that the grown-ups rejected the discovery at first because they didn't accept the odd dress of the astronomer. Could this have struck a chord with the pilot and brought him back to his childhood? When he presented drawing number one, his masterpiece of a boa constrictor that swallowed an animal whole, it was quickly rejected by grown-ups because he was a child and they labeled the drawing a hat.

The little prince thought that grown-ups often missed the most important aspects of life, like rejecting the great discovery of asteroid B-612 because of the way the astronomer dressed. People seem to focus on what's unimportant rather than on matters of great concern. The little prince give examples of that foolishness: inquiring how much a beautiful house costs rather than appreciating its inherent beauty, or asking not about a friend's likes or dislikes but about what his father does for a living and what socioeconomic status he and his family have achieved in life.[21] These kinds of reactions further support the position of the little prince that grown-ups only judge by outward appearances and fail to appreciate the true essence of the person or the object.

We have all heard the adage, "Never judge a book by its cover," but we all tend to do just that. We form an initial opinion of someone or something without understanding or knowing its true essence. Once we form these opinions, we are then linked even upon further discovery to conclusions which may be wrong. Did the pilot attach these conclusions to the appearance of the little prince? Would the pilot react to the little prince the same way the grown-ups reacted to his drawing number one? Would anyone ever believe that this small creature called the little prince actually existed? What would the pilot do to provide the necessary proofs that the little prince existed? Would proof be that he laughed, wore a blue cape, carried a sword, or asked for a sheep to be drawn? Would grown-ups be convinced of

---

[21] Saint-Exupéry, *The Little Prince*, p. 25.

his existence despite his odd appearance? Did he exist even if only in the pilot's imagination?

The Bible speaks to this particular problem of judging people, places and things only on the surface. Grown-ups fail to ascertain the more important essence of the object and the person to be known. The biblical story of Samuel and David is an example. When Samuel, as a prophet of Israel, was to select a king after the reign of the wicked Saul, he was directed by the Lord to go the house of Jesse. When Samuel arrived at the house of Jesse, he found that Jesse had eight sons. Samuel called for each of the sons to come before him, starting with the oldest and strongest. "And Jesse made seven of his sons pass before Samuel. And Samuel said to Jesse the Lord has not chosen these."[22] Samuel knew that the Lord would direct him on whom to anoint as King of Israel. So Samuel then asked Jesse whether he had any more sons. Jesse replied that the youngest, David, was in the field: "there remains yet the youngest, but he is keeping the sheep."[23] In the eyes of his father Jesse, David was just a child tending the sheep. But God rejected the other seven sons because God does not judge based on outward appearances of age and size, as Jesse did in not bringing forth the youngest of all his sons. Samuel judged on the inward aspects of the boy as directed by God: "God looks to the heart of man."[24] David was selected to be King of Israel by God.

Jesus condemned people's hypocrisy when they judged others from the outside based on how they look or how they dress:

> "Woe to you Scribes and Pharisees hypocrites! For you are like whitewashed tombs which outwardly appear beautiful but within are full of dead people's bones and all uncleanness. So, your outward appearance appears righteous to others, but within you are full of hypocrisy and lawlessness."[25]

---

[22] 1 Samuel 16:10 ESV.
[23] 1 Samuel 16:11 ESV.
[24] 1 Samuel 16:7 ESV.
[25] Matthew 23:27–28 ESV.

This judging by outward appearances is why the Turkish astronomer who had discovered asteroid B-612 and the pilot whose masterpiece was his first drawing were both rejected by the grown-ups.

As grown-ups, we must outgrow the ways we think and make judgments of people. If we do, then we will be able to see the animal eaten whole by the boa constrictor and not just see it as a hat or the sheep through the walls of the box. We shall see if the pilot is able to see the little prince for what he is and to understand the purpose of his visit in spite of his odd appearance. Will the pilot be able to see the important things of life and not judge by outward appearances?

Chapter 5

A Bad Tree

By their fruit you will recognize them. Do people pick grapes from thorn bushes or figs from trestles? Likewise, every good tree bears good fruit but every bad tree bears bad fruit.
Matthew 7:16–17 (NIV)

The little prince discloses to the pilot the main problem he has on his little planet, possibly asteroid B-612: baobabs, a most unruly and dangerous tree. Evidently these baobab trees existed on all planets. Much like the boa constrictor that ate the animal whole, as in the pilot's drawing number one, the baobab tree was capable of overtaking the little planet where the little prince lived by having its large roots overgrow or, even worse, split the planet in half. The little prince told the pilot that he once knew of somebody who allowed the baobabs to grow so large that they did overtake the planet and made it uninhabitable. This outcome would not be permitted by the little prince on his planet. The little prince said, "But when it is a bad plant, one must destroy it at all costs."[26] The little prince was diligent in his recognition of this most dangerous plant called the baobab. The little prince routinely monitored his planet for them and pulled them up before they could take root.

The most prized possession of the little prince was a rose that

---

[26] Saint-Exupéry, *The Little Prince*, p. 30.

he adored. The problem with these infectious baobabs is that they looked much like his beloved rose in the early stages of its growth. The little prince had to be careful not to pull out the wrong plant. So he carefully studied the budding of the plant, and once he identified that it was the dreaded baobab tree, he pulled it out so it didn't impact the good plants or his planet.

The baobab trees bring to mind two parables that Jesus taught, one on the wheat and tares, and the other on the tree and its fruit. In the parable of the tree and its fruit, Jesus instructed us to recognize the difference between the two: "Do people pick grapes from thorn bushes or figs from trestles? Likewise, every good tree bears good fruit, but a bad tree bears bad fruit."[27] The parable contemplates two different plants that look similar and grow together, but one was a good tree and the other was a bad tree. The little prince learned quickly to identify the good tree from the bad tree and dealt with the bad baobabs immediately.

In the parable of the wheat and the tares, Jesus explains:

> The kingdom of heaven is like a man who sowed good seed in his field. But while everyone was sleeping, his enemy came and sowed weeds among the wheat and went away. When the wheat sprouted and formed heads, then weeds also appeared.[28]

The little prince faced a problem with the baobabs much like Jesus's parable of the sower. A farmer went out to plant seeds on his property. The seeds fell on different soils. One of the soils on which the seeds fell was thorny, so that the plants were choked by thorns as they tried to grow, just as the little prince encountered the problem with the baobabs on his planet. And just as the baobab in its early stages looks like a rose, Jesus explained to his followers that the weeds looked similar to the wheat in this parable. The landowner was asked by his workers, "Should we pull them now?" The landowner replied,

---

[27] Matthew 7:16–17 NIV.
[28] Matthew 13:24–26 NIV.

"No, because while you are pulling the weeds, you may pull up the wheat with them. Let them both grow together until the harvest. At that time, I will tell the harvester first collect the weeds and tie them in bundles to be burned; then gather the wheat and bring them to my barn."[29] Jesus explained what these parables meant from a spiritual perspective.

The little prince, unlike others, hardly let the baobabs get to the point of the thorns and weeds in the parables. He was vigilant in knowing that the baobab trees were the enemy to him, his planet, and everything there. The little prince was very protective of his planet, and although these bad baobab trees would grow continuously from the ground, he was vigilant in not allowing them to take root and continue to grow so that they impacted his planet. He said, "You must see to it that you pull up regularly the baobabs, at the very first moment when they are to be distinguished from the rose bushes they resemble so closely in their earliest years."[30]

What does this all mean? Was there a spiritual or theological message hidden within the baobab trees? The little prince suggested "in consequence there were good seeds from good plants and bad seeds from bad plants, but bad seeds can't produce good plants."[31] Jesus explained the principle of the parables: the one who sowed the good seeds was the Son of Man. The field is the world, and the good seeds stand for the sons of the kingdom. The weeds are the sons of the evil one, and the enemy who sows them is the devil.[32]

Here on the little prince's planet, possibly B-612, is the cosmic spiritual struggle of good versus evil in the baobab trees. Even the little prince has to deal with the concepts of life and death, good and evil. In fact, that struggle may be present on every planet in the universe.

---

[29] Matthew 13:29-30 NIV.
[30] Saint-Exupéry, *The Little Prince*, p. 32.
[31] Saint-Exupéry, *The Little Prince*, p. 30.
[32] Matthew 13:37-39 NIV.

Chapter 6

A Sad Life

The Lord is near to the brokenhearted and saves the crushed in spirit.
Psalm 34:18 (ESV)

Life is full of complexities, sorrow, and unhappiness. When we can experience joy or happiness from external circumstances, we should embrace them, as they come few and far between. Rather, we are consumed with the struggles of this world, the pressures from life's circumstances, anxiety, suffering, and loss.

The pilot came to the understanding that the little prince lived a very sad life. This understanding was a bit of a surprise, considering the little prince's jovial outward disposition. But underneath all the laughter and all the perceived happiness was a very sad little creature. The pilot was able to discern that the only true happiness the little prince experienced was watching sunsets.

One day it was reported that the little prince saw over forty sunsets from his little planet, possibly asteroid B-612. During this time, the little prince observed the sunsets covered the sadness, even if only momentarily. The Bible speaks to the issue of sadness. The psalmist wrote of his lament, "The Lord is near the brokenhearted and saves the crushed in spirit."

The author of the Old Testament book of Deuteronomy writes,

"He will never leave you or forsake you."[33] These verses are important to remember when we go through life's difficult circumstances. Promises from God that he will never abandon us must become true to us during those trying times. More importantly, Jesus proclaimed in the greatest sermon ever preached, the Sermon on the Mount, "Blessed are the poor in spirit, for theirs is the kingdom of heaven. Blessed are those who mourn for they will be comforted."[34] The principle of sorrow and sadness is part of the human condition—and it is not only a part of the human condition but inherent in the universe in which we live. Even the creature called the little prince was not outside sadness, loss, good, and evil on his own little planet.

We are promised by God in our human condition—whether it be mourning, sadness, or sorrow—that there is hope in the midst of suffering. That hope is found in something outside ourselves. The little prince found comfort in seeing a beautiful sunset time and time again. We need to look outside ourselves for comfort in times of sadness. This is a very peculiar lesson that we have learned from the little prince, and an unexpected one. In life, sorrow and sadness are inevitable. In one of the most significant scriptures, the suffering servant in Isaiah[35] contemplates a messiah who would have a life of sorrows and suffering for others: "He was despised and rejected by men, a man of sorrows, and familiar with suffering."[36] If the Messiah would go through this, being God, how would we be spared?

That scripture foreshadowed the life and suffering of Jesus Christ and his identity, as the Gospel of John confirms that Jesus of Nazareth was the suffering servant, though "even after Jesus had done all these miraculous signs in their presence; they still would not believe in him." Fulfilling the words of Isaiah the prophet, Jesus was often referred to as a man of sorrows although he was God in the flesh![37] Jesus of Nazareth is further confirmed as the suffering servant in the

---

[33] Deuteronomy 31:8.
[34] Matthew 5:3–4 NIV.
[35] Isaiah 53.
[36] Isaiah 53:3 NIV.
[37] John 12:37-38 NIV.

book of Acts: "he was led like a sheep to the slaughter and as a lamb before its shearer for he did not open his mouth."[38]

Once again I am reminded of the little prince's sheep in Jesus, the Lamb of God, a perfect sacrifice for humanity's sins, through which we may learn that suffering, sorrow, and sadness is a necessary part of the human condition, with eternal implications. Suffering, sorrow, and death cannot be looked at it in a vacuum. The Old Testament figure Job was quick to point out, "Shall we receive good from God, and shall we not receive evil?"[39] It appears the little prince was keenly aware of this principle and looked for a time of laughter and restoration. Would the pilot also find this?

---

[38] Acts 8:32 NIV.
[39] Job 2:10 ESV.

Chapter 7

One Flower Unique in All the World

I am a rose of Sharon, a lily of the valleys.
Like a lily among thorns is my darling among the young women.
Song of Solomon 2:1–2 (NIV)

We now encounter the little prince's rose. Roses are often identified as standing for the proposition of love and sacrifice. William Shakespeare wrote, "What's in a name? That which we call a rose by any other name would smell as sweet." Other quotes about roses I'm drawn to are two of anonymous authorship:

> A life filled with love, must have some thorns, but a
> life empty of love will have no roses.

> There are many flowers in life … but only one rose.

And this is where I will pick up the story of the little prince and his rose.

The pilot in this passage of *The Little Prince* believes he learns more about this little creature called the little prince than he had known previously. The little prince discloses that he has important concerns about the sheep the pilot drew for him while the pilot was consumed by and preoccupied with fixing his airplane and surviving. The little prince worries that if or when he takes the sheep back to his planet (remember, possibly asteroid B-612), the sheep may eat his rose. The little prince feels that would be a terrible and tragic event!

It was of the utmost importance to the little prince that the rose be protected. The pilot called this "the secret of the little prince's life."[40] The little prince was so concerned that in an instant the sheep could eat his rose. The little prince initially thought the thorns would deter the sheep from eating the rose, but that hope was quickly dashed by the pilot. In no uncertain terms, the pilot told the little prince that thorns would not protect the rose from the sheep. The little prince was incredulous; he could not understand why the rose would have such a complex and potent defense system but be unable to fully protect herself. When the little prince asked why, to satisfy the questioner the pilot initially said the first thing that came into his mind: "The rose only has thorns for spite."[41]

The little prince was very upset, to say the least, that his rose would be unprotected from the sheep. The pilot realized his statement had caused the little prince great anxiety, so he decided to formulate a resolution. He drew a muzzle on the sheep so it could not eat the rose, and for additional protection around the rose he drew a fence so others also would not be able to harm the rose. This resolution seemed to satisfy the little prince.

This issue of why roses have thorns caused the little prince to become so angry and upset that there was almost no consoling him. The little prince then told of a person he had met on another planet, a red-faced gentleman called the accountant, who only would add figures on his calculator. He would tell the little prince that he was concerned with "matters of consequence."[42] The little prince felt that figures were not matters of consequence! His rose, especially the protection of his unique rose, was a matter of consequence. The little prince felt grown-ups like the pilot and the accountant failed to

---

[40] Saint-Exupéry, *The Little Prince*, p. 37.
[41] Saint-Exupéry, *The Little Prince*, p. 38.
[42] Saint-Exupéry, *The Little Prince*, p. 39.

see the importance of something that has happened for millions of years—roses being eaten by sheep.[43]

The little prince even feared that if his rose was eaten by a sheep, the universe and stars would go dark. This was clearly a matter of the greatest importance to the little prince. The pilot reassured the little creature that he would take every precaution to keep the unique rose, his rose, safe from the sheep.

Why all this concern over a rose, you may ask? Of all the flowers in the world, why a rose? A rose has biblical meaning. Isaiah 35 reveals a beautiful picture of the king and blessings on his return home:

> The wilderness are in the solitary place shall be pride for them and the desert shall rejoice for them, and blossom as the rose. It shall blossom abundantly and rejoice even with joy and singing, the glory of Lebanon shall be given unto it, the excellency of Carmel and Sharon, they shall see the glory of the Lord, and the excellency of our God.[44]

The beauty and majesty of the rose make it fit to celebrate a king. The Song of Solomon says, "I am a rose of Sharon, a lily of the valleys."[45] This is the first reference to a rose in the Bible. In ancient Christian communities, roses were taken to symbolize God's worth in our lives, and in Catholic symbolism possibly the shedding of Christ's blood. The red rose may also symbolize God's unconditional and uncommon love for humanity, much like the love the little prince had for his rose and the love expressed in the Song of Solomon for the beloved. Christ has been compared to a rose for its red color, which may be expressive of the truth of humanity and his bloody sufferings in it. The word "rose" denotes a type of shrub and particularly its flower, which appears in the Bible twice, once in

---

[43] Saint-Exupéry, *The Little Prince*, p. 40.
[44] Isaiah 3:1–2 NIV.
[45] Solomon 2:1 NIV.

the Song of Solomon 2:1, where the rose of Sharon represents beauty, and in in Isaiah 35:1–2, where a beautiful flower blossoms, though not specifically a rose.[46]

The Christian life to a degree replicates that of a rose. It is beautiful and fragrant in times of birth, joy and happiness. It has thorns, which represent life's trying circumstances, difficulties, and death. Fittingly, when Jesus was crucified, the soldiers twisted a crown of thorns and put it on his head.[47] We don't know what plant or bush these thorns were from, but we know what the thorns stood for, and what the little prince believed, "that the thorns are terrible weapons,"[48] is precisely the role they played. But every rose has its thorns, and every thorn has its rose!

The little prince discusses his rose at length. It may be that life has its great beauty, joy, and happiness, which the beautiful color and fragrance of the rose would signify. But there is also pain, suffering, tragedy, and difficult circumstances, which the thorns of the rose may signify. We are challenged to traverse this thing we call life, but we take comfort in knowing that while this life, like the lifespan of a rose, is transient, we have eternity to look forward to, as the little prince does.

As the writer of Ecclesiastes puts it,

> He has made everything beautiful in its time period he has also set eternity in the hearts of men; that yet, they cannot fathom what God has done from the beginning to the end.[49]

This may not only be our hope, but also that of the little prince.

---

[46] "Song of Solomon 2:1," John Gill's Exposition of the Bible, Bible Study Tools.com, https://www.biblestudytools.com/commentaries/gills-exposition-of-the-bible/song-of-solomon-2-1.html, accessed November 27, 2023.
[47] John 19:2 NIV.
[48] Saint-Exupéry, *The Little Prince*, p. 38.
[49] Ecclesiastes 3:11 NIV.

Chapter 8

Vanity of Vanities

"Vanity of vanities," says the Preacher,
"vanities of vanities, all is vanity."
Ecclesiastes 1:2 (NASV)

We now learn one of the reasons the little prince may have left his own planet, which we have been identifying as possibly asteroid B-612. It may have been, in fact, because of love. The little prince suggests to the pilot that he left his planet because he was unable to understand or deal with the vanity of his rose. Although he loved his rose, he described for the pilot the issues he had with the rose and just how he came to meet the rose. It happened one day when the wind blew a seed onto the planet of the little prince. He did not know how the seed got there but was concerned that it might be a seedling from the notorious baobab plants, so he watched it with great concern.[50]

When the plant finally sprouted, it was not a baobab but a beautiful, fragrant rose. Immediately the demands of the rose from being beautiful and fragrant caused great torment to the little prince. He was ill-equipped to deal with such beauty and vanity, which he had not experienced previously. It appeared from the demands of this beautiful rose that she needed protection and warmth. These were of

---

[50] Saint-Exupéry, *The Little Prince*, p. 43.

importance to the rose, and she showed little concern or care for the little prince's own needs.

The little prince took care of this beautiful rose, making sure the rose was always comfortable and protected. But she would continually disrupt the little prince with her unruly demands and statements of anger. The little prince would tend to her every need each day, watering her and ensuring that she was comfortable, preserved, and protected. The rose's conduct began to weigh heavily on the little prince, until finally he decided to leave her and his planet for good!

Merriam-Webster defines *vanity* as "inflated pride in oneself or one's appearance."[51] Now, the little prince would never believe the rose was valueless for he knew she had great beauty and dispersed a beautiful aroma all over his planet. But the issue the little prince had with the rose was that she was so demanding and unconcerned with his needs.

The Bible speaks to the dangers of vanity. This is an example of why Jesus taught that the Greatest Commandment was not only to love, serve, and obey God with all your heart, soul, mind, and strength, but to love your neighbor as yourself and do unto others as you would have done to you.[52] In the Gospel of Matthew, Jesus explains the importance of treating others with respect, equality, and love. Certainly in the mind of the little prince, the rose was so consumed with herself and her own needs that she never considered anyone else.

In the Bible, Jesus was confronted by the religious leaders of his day. They conspired to test or trap Jesus with a question: "Teacher, which is the greatest commandment in the law? They knew there were hundreds, but Jesus replied,

> Love the Lord your God with all your heart, and with all your soul, and with all your mind, and strength. This is the first and the greatest commandment. And the second is like it. Love your neighbor as yourself.[53]

---

[51] Merriam-Webster online, s.v. "vanity," https://www.merriam-webster.com/dictionary/vanity, accessed November 27, 2023.
[52] Matthew 22:36–40 NIV.
[53] Matthew 22:37–39 NIV.

Certainly, these biblical concepts initially were foreign to the rose, she was so consumed with her own vanity and beauty to the detriment of the little prince. The little prince sacrificed his own well-being and peace of mind for the rose, and it ultimately led to him leaving his own planet. Although he never stopped loving the rose or being concerned for her, he could no longer tolerate her.

Saint Paul in a letter to the church at Corinth warned the people about vanity and pursuing their own desires and relegating the needs of others as the rose did. He wrote:

> Everything is permissible, but not everything is beneficial. Everything is permissible, but not everything is constructive. Nobody should seek his own good but the good of others.[54]

These are good moral standards to live by.

Seeking the good of another was precisely what the little prince did in his relationship with his rose, but the rose failed to reciprocate. One of the great directives the Lord Jesus gave was, "Greater love hath no man than this that a man lay down his life for his friends,"[55] and that is what the little prince did daily for the rose. Certainly, love and sacrifice such as this were not in the equation of how the rose treated the little prince. The rose was not able to do so because of her own vanity and self-centeredness. She was unable to treat the little prince the way she wanted to be treated.

I don't know if the little prince ever learned this lesson fully, although he showed great love and concern for the well-being of the rose. In the end the little prince believed, "I ought to have judged by deeds and not by words. She cast her fragrance and her radiance over me. I ought never to have run away from her."[56]

Regret is heavy to live with, as our little friend would learn.

---

[54] 1 Corinthians 10:23–24 NIV.
[55] John 15:13 KJV.
[56] Saint-Exupéry, *The Little Prince*, p. 48.

Chapter 9

Forgiveness

If we confess our sins he is faithful and just to forgive us our sins, and to cleanse us from all unrighteousness.
1 John 1:9 (KJV)

The decision of the little prince to leave his planet, which may have been asteroid B-612, was fraught with emotion. The little prince decided nothing was going to change his mind about leaving even the rose. On the last day the little prince was on his planet, he got all his normal chores done, cleaned out the three volcanoes (two of which were active), watered his rose, and tidied his area of the planet. He pulled out the last remaining baobab trees. But since the planet was infested by the plant, it was only a matter of time before they overran the planet and put everything in jeopardy, including his rose.

The little prince was not planning on ever returning to his little planet. After he completed all his tasks, he said goodbye to his rose. The rose, who had so much vanity and self-concern, said something that took the little prince by surprise. "I have been silly. I ask your forgiveness. Try to be happy ... of course I love you, and it is my fault that you have not known it all the while."[57]

The rose's statement is consistent with biblical teaching on achieving forgiveness for our sins.

---

[57] Saint-Exupéry, *The Little Prince*, p. 50.

> If you have sinned you should tell each other what you have done. Then you can pray for one another and be healed. The prayer of an innocent person is powerful and it can help a lot.[58]

This turn of events was shocking to the little prince, given the rose's prior treatment of him. It was the first time in their relationship that the rose had considered the little prince's feelings and his needs. The rose realized that she had acted selfishly and in vanity, and asked the little prince to forgive her. The little prince never responded to what she said, probably out of shock or disbelief. She then told him to go, which he had already decided to do.

But before the little prince left his little planet, he wanted to make sure his rose would be protected, comfortable, and not too cold. He offered the rose a glass dome that could be put over her so she would not be cold. She rejected his offer, saying that she would be fine and would need to acclimate to life now without the little prince taking care of her every need.

Just as the little prince was ready to leave his planet, he came upon a flock of birds that happened to be passing by his little planet. In that moment, he took advantage of the flock of birds to make his departure.[59]

Regret oftentimes is difficult and painful to deal with. When somebody acts a certain way and that conduct affects another's well-being, the pain may leave deep wounds. Not all regret is bad. We see here in the case of the rose that through regret she acknowledged her conduct and wrongdoing, and was truly sorry for how she acted. She even asked forgiveness from the one she offended, that being the little prince.

The Bible has similar tenets. The Apostle Paul wrote on this subject to the church:

> Even if I caused you sorrow by my letter, I do not regret it. Though I did regret it—I see that my letter

---

[58] James 5:16 CEV.
[59] Saint-Exupéry, *The Little Prince*, p. 49.

hurt you but only for a little while—yet now I am happy because your sorrow leads you to repentance. For you became sorrowful as God intended.[60]

The Apostle Paul depicts a spiritual process that the rose experienced when she acted improperly, regretted it, then asked for forgiveness. The rose was regretful for how she had acted and attempted to make things right. This acknowledgment leads to blessings of all parties and a lifting of the weight of regret from both the offender and the offended. Saint Paul continued, saying that "godly sorrow brings repentance that leads to salvation and leaves no regret."[61] Is this what the rose and the little prince experienced in this moment? We will never know, but we do know that when the little prince left his planet, possibly asteroid B-612, both he and the rose had made peace with each other, and there were no regrets.

When the rose asked forgiveness for her attitude and conduct, it was a paradigm shift in the progression of *The Little Prince*. Up to that point, the little prince was tormented by the demands of the rose, and he could no longer endure those hardships. An aspect of experiencing the emotion of regret that wasn't considered is its natural effect or consequence on the individuals. If we look to scripture, we can see numerous times people have regretted the way they acted and the decisions they made. This is part of the human condition. As early as the first book of the Bible, Genesis, "God saw that the wickedness of man was great in the earth, and that every imagination of the thoughts of his heart was only evil continually. And it repented the Lord that he made man on the earth and it grieved him to his heart."[62]

We have seen how regret and recognizing one's sin can lead to healing and restoration of both parties. And we can see regret having a positive effect on one of Jesus's disciples, that being Peter, who we know even denied knowing Christ three times. After Peter had proclaimed his undying love and commitment to Jesus, Jesus told

---

[60] 2 Corinthians 7:8–11.
[61] 2 Corinthians 7:10 NIV.
[62] Genesis 6:5–6 KJV.

him, "You will deny three times that you know me."[63] After Jesus was arrested, Peter was confronted with the allegation that he too was a follower or disciple of this Jesus. That is when Peter denied he ever knew Christ. Thereafter, the regret Peter underwent led him to realize his wrongdoing by denying the Lord who had loved him, so much so that he "went outside and wept bitterly."[64] This is a positive result when one recognizes their faults and regrets their conduct and repents of it. We know also of the one disciple who betrayed Jesus for thirty pieces of silver and was so seized with remorse that "he went away and hanged himself,"[65] but his regret came too late.

---

[63] Luke 22:34 NIV.
[64] Luke 22:62 NIV.
[65] Matthew 27:5 NIV.

Chapter 10

The King

*In the Lord's hand the King's heart is a stream of water
that he channels towards all who please him.*
Proverbs 21:1 (NIV)

    The little prince, having left his planet, is now on his celestial journey through the universe. He makes his first stop in his travels, which ultimately will end in going to Earth. The first character the little prince meets after leaving his planet is a king. This king evidently rules a small planet with nothing or no one on it—no castles, no subjects—at least until the arrival of the little prince. The king knew or had heard of the little prince already but had never met him. Would the little prince be the king's first subject?

    The king appeared to the little prince to be somewhat of a reasonable king, judging from his initial directives and orders. The little prince commented, "Although he was an absolute monarch, but because he was a good man, he made his orders reasonable."[66] During the colloquy between the king and the little prince, the little prince learned that the king's authority was not much authority after all. The king commanded things that would be or had already been established or that would occur. Thereafter the king issued an order in conformance to that event. Ordering things that are going to happen

---

[66] Saint-Exupéry, *The Little Prince*, p. 56.

on their own anyway was very confusing to the little prince—it seemed to undermine the true power and authority of the king.

The king explained that he ruled over everything in the universe and did not accept any insubordination. The little prince wondered how the king obtained seemingly unlimited power and authority. Where did it come from, and was it even real? When the little prince asked the king with so-called absolute power and authority, one who rules and does not tolerate insubordination, to order the sun to set so he could see a sunset, the king quickly realized he couldn't, so he consulted an almanac to determine precisely when the sun would set and then gave the order at that time. The king had no true power or authority to order anything. His power and authority was just an illusion.

The king did not want the little prince to leave his tiny planet but rather wanted him to be his first real subject. So he offered the little prince a job as Minister of Justice. The little prince responded that there was no one on the planet to judge. That was when the king dispensed pearls of wisdom to the little prince. "Then you shall judge yourself," the king answered. "That is the most difficult thing of all. It is much more difficult to judge oneself than to judge others."[67]

Wisdom from the Bible confirms this concept. The book of Lamentations says, "Let us examine and probe our ways, and let us return to the Lord,"[68] and Galatians says, "But each one must exam his own work, and then you will have reason for boasting for himself and not in relation to another."[69]

The king tried to convince the little prince to stay on his planet and be of service. The king wished that the little prince would take the job that was offered. The only other inhabitant of the planet outside themselves was a common rat. The king told the little prince that as part of his job as Minister of Justice, he would condemn the rat to death but then pardon him each time, as he was the only other living creature on this planet.[70]

---

[67] Saint-Exupéry, *The Little Prince*, pp. 59–60.
[68] Lamentations 3:40 NIV.
[69] Lamentations 6:4 NIV.
[70] Saint-Exupéry, *The Little Prince*, p. 60.

The little prince was not convinced. He rejected the offer, having realized that this planet was not for him. His visit was short, and he would soon leave.

This exchange between the little prince and the king raised the question of true authority. It reminds me of the exchange Jesus had with the religious leaders who questioned him as to where his authority had come from. Jesus correctly proclaimed, "All authority in heaven and earth has been given to me."[71] Similarly, in contrast to what Jesus said to Pilate before he was condemned to death, "You would have no authority over me at all unless it had been given to you from above."[72] Jesus was explaining that true authority originates from God.

Although the little prince understood the meaning of true authority and power and believed the king had none, the king had still been able to dispense some nuggets of wisdom to the little prince.

The subject of judging oneself is a very important spiritual concept. The Bible speaks in several areas of judging ourselves and others. The Apostle Paul directed the church on the proper way to take communion, the elements of communion being the body and blood of Our Lord represented in wine and bread. Before believers partake of the elements of communion, Paul directs us to "examine ourselves before we eat of the bread and drink of the cup. For anyone who eats and drinks without recognizing the body of the Lord eats and drinks judgment upon themselves."[73] This means that we are to reflect on our inherent sin and shortcomings in our own lives so we can be right with God and others before we partake of the elements.

Self-reflection is important to human or creaturely existence, as we have seen demonstrated by the rather regretful conduct of the little prince's rose. Jesus also warned the people to be careful about judging others: "Do not judge or you too will be judged in the same way you judge others you will be judged, and with the measure you use it will be measured to you."[74]

---

[71] Matthew 28:18 NIV.
[72] John 19:11 ESV.
[73] 1 Corinthians 11:28 NIV.
[74] Matthew 7:1–2 NIV.

Although the king had no inherent power or authority, the wisdom and principles dispensed by him should be taken to heart. As he said, the most difficult person to judge is oftentimes ourselves, and this theme echoes the teachings of Christ.

> Why do you look at the speck of sawdust in your brother's eye and pay no attention to the plank in your own eye? How can you say to your brother, let me take the speck out of your eye, when all the time there is a plank in your own eye? ... First take the plank out of your own eye and then you will see clearly to remove the speck out of your brother's eye.[75]

This parable describes the correct process of judgment, whether of ourselves or others, much like the chapter from *The Little Prince* about the king. The king's wisdom to judge ourselves first is very much like that of Jesus.

We must be able to see ourselves objectively and clearly. We cannot do that if we have a log or plank in our eye blocking our spiritual view. It is not how we perceive ourselves but how we actually are. Once we come to understand our own shortcomings and "remove the plank," we can acknowledge and hopefully correct them. Only then shall we see clearly enough to remove the splinter from our brother's eye. This valuable teaching was worth the stop the little prince made to the king's planet, even if it was for a very brief time.

---

[75] Matthew 7:3–5 NIV.

Chapter 11

Clap Your Hands for Me

For if anyone thinks he is something when he is nothing, he deceives himself.
Galatians 6:3 (NIV)

The second planet that the little prince visits towards his unknown travel to Earth has just one inhabitant. It is a lone man with a funny hat. When the little prince was on his way, the man saw him from a distance and figured "an admirer is coming to visit here." As soon as the little prince arrived, the man asked him to clap his hands.[76] *What an odd request*, the little prince thought, but he complied. What was the reason for this strange request?

When the little prince began to clap his hands, the man raised his hat off his head as if he was royalty to salute the crowd of one. The little prince marveled at this and thought it entertaining and funny, so he continued to clap. When he clapped the man, tipped his hat again! But what did it all mean?

The man asked the little prince if he admired him and told the little prince in no uncertain terms that he was the "richest and most intelligent man on the planet."[77] True, he was the only one on the planet. The little prince appeared to act with knowledge and wisdom,

---

[76] Saint–Exupéry, *The Little Prince*, p. 62.
[77] Saint–Exupéry, *The Little Prince*, p. 64.

and displayed more self-control than this arrogant man who sought out unwarranted admiration. The little prince would quickly grow tired of this man's antics and attitude.

The Bible calls this kind of a man a fool. "Do you see a man wise in his own ways and his own eyes? There is more hope for a fool than for him."[78] That appears to be the impression left on the little prince by the man with the hat.

Jesus also taught about several conceited men by parables. One parable begins when Jesus was confronted with a legal issue about inheritance between two brothers, who were arguing about which one should receive what portion. Jesus warned them first "to be on guard against all kinds of greed."[79] He then offered this parable:

> The ground of a certain rich man produced a good crop. He thought to himself, "What shall I do? I have a place to store my crops." Then he said, "This is what I'll do. I will tear down my barns and build bigger ones, and there I will store my surplus grain. And I'll say to myself, 'You have plenty of grain laid up for many years. Take life easy; eat, drink and be merry.' "[80]

This appears to be the attitude and objective of many people in society today.

So often I hear of people wanting to have enough money to retire, not work, and move here or there. Unfortunately, we fail to contemplate the transitory nature of life and death. We fail to consider that life can change in an instant, and all our plans and objectives become like the wind. This lesson is important for us to learn and understand not only for this life but the life to come. The parable of the rich fool concludes "God said to him, 'You fool! This

---

[78] Proverbs 26:12 NIV.
[79] Luke 12:15 NIV.
[80] Luke 12:16–19 NIV.

very night your life will be demanded from you and who will get what you have prepared for yourself?' "[81] This is the harsh reality of life.

An accompanying parable picks up where the parable of the rich fool left off—a parable about the transition from life to death, or rather eternity. The Bible tells us that in a flash, in one moment, in an instant, in the blink of an eye, we will be transformed from this temporal life to eternity. So the question is, what happens after this temporal life? Much of it depends on how we as creatures acted and reacted in the time that we lived.

We just read the parable that Jesus gave about the rich fool who never contemplated his own mortality but rather was consumed with pride, arrogance, and conceit of what he accomplished in life. It did not end well for him. In this parable, we see and have a glimpse of the afterlife. Jesus introduced us to these concepts in the parable of another rich man and the beggar Lazarus. In this parable, Jesus depicts a rich man much like the "eat, drink, and be merry" one, or maybe the same one.

This rich man had all the trappings of a luxurious and comfortable life when the beggar Lazarus did not. Now in the afterlife, the rich man is experiencing suffering, torment, and unquenchable thirst in hell. The rich man sees the poor beggar he knew by the name of Lazarus, who by all accounts suffered in life with physical pain, sores, and a lack of food. The poor beggar Lazarus was a pitiful soul in life. In juxtaposition to the comfortable life of the rich man, Lazarus had very little. The parable goes on to say Lazarus would beg from the rich man's own table to be fed. Now the roles have been reversed.

Lazarus lived a very difficult and tormented existence in his life. But through all the pain, suffering, and difficult circumstances that Lazarus experienced, he not only loved God but was loved by God. It is hard to reconcile the good suffering so much with nothing and the evil prospering, but that is precisely what we have here. It must be realized that in our life and all its circumstances, suffering is temporary, in contrast with eternity, which is forever. We know this

---

[81] Luke 12:20 NIV.

because scripture tells us that when it was time for Lazarus to die, "angels carried him to Abraham's side."[82] Abraham's bosom was a place of peace, tranquility, and comfort, in contrast to the rich man who now lived in constant torment, burning, pain, and suffering—the biblical picture of hell.

The conditions were so bad that the rich man asked Lazarus to bring him relief by just dipping his finger in a cup of water to quench his thirst. This was not possible; the rich man and Lazarus were separated by a huge spiritual chasm that could not be crossed. Those in the paradise of Abraham's bosom could not and would not cross over to hell, nor could the reverse occur, owing to the rich fools' lifetime of conceit, arrogance, and unbelief.

The little prince was able to discern quickly that the character of this man with the hat was quite prideful. *This is no planet for me*, he thought and immediately left.

---

[82] Luke 16:22 NIV.

Chapter 12

The Tippler

Woe to those who rise early in the morning, that may run after strong drink, who tarry late into the evening as wine enflames them!
Isaiah 5:11 (EVS)

This may be the most uninteresting chapter in *The Little Prince*, but yet it has significance to culture today and may serve a useful purpose. The next planet the little prince visits seems to appear out of thin air. He visits this planet very briefly but is very disturbed with its only inhabitant. That inhabitant is a man called a tippler. We don't use this phrase or description nowadays, but a tippler is one who indulges in the excessive drinking of alcohol.

The little prince discerned that the tippler was drinking to forget his own condition. He drank to excess, littering his planet with empty bottles he had already drunk and full bottles yet to be consumed. The little prince was greatly disturbed by the conduct and the demeanor of the tippler, and left the planet quickly—it may have been his shortest visit yet.

The Bible contains many scriptures on the subject of alcohol. Drinking alcohol is considered by many to be contrary to the Christian faith, but I believe this concern is often misplaced. Certainly, the Bible warns about overindulgence in alcohol and drunkenness, but some passages suggest that in certain situations drinking alcohol is permissible. In 1 Timothy 5:23, Paul encourages Timothy to use a little wine for his stomach condition. Although that instance may be true, let us look collectively at scriptures that reference alcohol and drinking.

Whether to drink or abstain from alcohol has long been debated among various Christian sects. Some believe that any and all drinking of alcoholic substances should be avoided at all costs. Other groups believe drinking alcohol is permissible. Although I personally do not drink and never have drunk alcohol, the Bible is less clear than many would want to believe. Certainly, there are scriptures that suggest drunken debauchery is against the tenants of the Christian faith and practice and would be a sin.

> For you have spent enough time in the past doing what pagans do living in debauchery, lust, drunkenness, orgies, carousing in detestable idolatries.[83]

> Do not get drunk on wine, which leads to debauchery, instead be filled with the spirit.[84]

> Wine is a mocker and beer a brawler whoever is led astray by them is not wise.[85]

These directives are aimed at people like the tippler who drink to get drunk or drink excessively.

We often forget that the first miracle Jesus performed was turning water into wine. (And no, it wasn't grape juice or colored water.) It is the first miracle that Jesus performed, recorded in John's gospel only. The miracle begins by Jesus attending a wedding feast at Cana with friends and family, including his mother, Mary. It appears that the host of the wedding was a family member or close friend. Now, either the guests drank too much or the host just failed to account for the number of guests and how much they would drink, but they ran out

---

[83] 1 Peter 4:3 NIV.
[84] Ephesians 5:18 NIV.
[85] Proverbs 20:1 NIV.

of wine. In Jesus's day and culture, running out of wine would reflect poorly on the family of the married couple and be dishonorable to the family. Mary, understanding the importance of this hospitality and the embarrassment the lack of wine would cause, approached her eldest son, Jesus and said, "They have no more wine."

Up to this point, Jesus had not performed a miracle. Mary knew he was the Son of God, whether or not she was mindful of this fact in the moment. At first Jesus protested and said, "My time has not yet come."[86]

Seemingly his mother did not consider his response, which indicated that he was apprehensive and not prepared to do a miracle. She simply instructed the servants to do whatever he told them to do. With those directives from his mother, Jesus told the servants to fill the jars with water. Then he told them, "Now draw some out and take it to the master of the banquet."[87] As it turned out, this wine miraculously created by Jesus was better than the wine that had been served at the wedding up to this point and was a great endorsement for the host.

Why was this the first miracle Jesus performed? We do not know the reasons or understand the mind of God—the opportunity simply may have presented itself, or since his own mother asked him, Jesus did the miracle to save her friends and family embarrassment. This miracle is a very special miracle in that it was done at the request of his mother, in fact the only miracle recorded as having been requested of Jesus by Mary. It hearkens back to Jesus's infancy and childhood, when Mary experienced all the special aspects of his birth and growth: "But Mary, treasured of all those things and pondered them in her heart."[88]

So it would be hard to adopt the position that drinking alcohol is against the tenets of the Christian faith. We also must consider that wine was an element used at the Last Supper "to represent the blood

---

[86] John 2:3–4 NIV.
[87] John 2:8 NIV.
[88] John 2:19 NIV.

of Christ that will be shed for our sins, and the bread that is used to represent his body broken for us."[89] One must be careful not to get drunk like the tippler, as is warned in the Bible. Paul further reminds us to consider others in our conduct: "It is not good to eat meat, or drink wine or to do anything by which your brother stumbles."[90]

Certainly, the little prince was not impressed; he was greatly disturbed by the conduct and attitude of the tippler. Would Jesus be concerned by our conduct today and quickly leave our planet?

---

[89] 1 Corinthians 11:23–26 NIV.
[90] Romans 14:20 NIV.

Chapter 13

The Poor Rich Businessman

*Keep your life free from love of money,
and be content with what you have.*
Hebrews 13:5 (NIV)

    The Bible has numerous scriptures that relate to the concept of money. The subject of money may in fact be even more referred to than categories of faith and prayer. Sixteen out of the thirty-eight parables deal with the topic of money and/or stewardship, second only to Jesus speaking on the kingdom of God. You may find it troubling that Jesus spoke so often about money, finances, and stewardship, but it may be because of the "inherent connection between a person's spiritual life, attitudes, and actions concerning money and possessions."[91]

    In this chapter, on his fourth planet the little prince meets a businessman, who is so preoccupied with his own business that he hardly notices the little prince's arrival. The businessman claims he is so busy counting all his wealth that he has no time for things and talk of no consequence. The little prince is perplexed by the businessman and his belief that counting the stars in the galaxy would somehow

---

[91] "Bible Verses about Money and Stewardship," Envoy Financial, https://www.envoyfinancial.com/participantresources/bible-verses-about-money-and-stewardship, accessed April 1, 2023.

create his wealth. How could the businessman own the stars? The little prince thinks, *That's impossible!* To own something you must have possession of it and interact with it, as he did his rose on his home planet. He had cared for the rose, protected it, and watered it each day. He had three volcanoes, two of which were active and one of which was not, but nevertheless he cleaned them all each day. He also had to deal with the baobab trees that threatened to take over his planet by growing so large.

By contrast, the businessman had nothing in his possession. The businessman was consumed with greed. It was imaginary greed to onlookers but real to him. Jesus warned the people, "Watch out! Be on your guard against all kinds of greed; a man's life does not consist in the abundance of his possessions."[92] The little prince did not believe the businessman owned or possessed "five hundred and one million, six hundred twenty-two thousand, seven hundred and thirty-one stars."[93] The businessman *thought* he owned all the stars, and in his mind he was one of the most significant, important, and wealthy people in all the universe. His perceived ownership of these 501,522,731 stars was tied to his whole persona. The identity of the businessman lay in the false security of that which he thought he owned. The Bible warns us, "Whoever trusts in his riches will fall, but the righteous will thrive like a green leaf."[94]

The conduct of the businessman reflects some of society's objectives and values to get or be rich. Look at that objective: in 2022, Americans spent $105.26 billion on lottery tickets, making the lottery the most popular form of gambling in the United States.[95] Many aspire to be or get rich, like the businessman, a hoarder of wealth—though in his case, he really didn't own anything but he

---

[92] Luke 12:15 NIV.
[93] Saint-Exupéry, *The Little Prince*, p. 68.
[94] Proverbs 11:28 NIV.
[95] Matthew Woodward, "Lottery Statistics: How Many People Play Lottery in the US?" Search Logistics, updated August 14, 2023, https://www.searchlogistics.com/learn/statistics/lottery-statistics, accessed November 27, 2023.

acted as though he did. Is this like today's Instagrammers, TikTokers, and YouTubers?

Jesus tells a parable about the trappings and pursuit of wealth. In the parable of the servants, a master entrusted three servants with his assets when he went away on a long trip. He gave each of the servants money to invest so that when he returned, his wealth would have increased even in his absence. Two of the servants wisely invested the money, and it grew, so when the master came back, he was greatly pleased. But one servant was so consumed with worries about money and the fear that he would not be able to utilize his abilities to make it grow that he buried it in the soil, and it did nothing. Needless to say, the master was angered at the mentality of the servant who did nothing with the investment. He took it back from him and gave it to the others who had multiplied the original investment.

We must be on guard against the desire for riches. I have met people with little or no resources who were consumed with money and wealth just like the businessman. I have met with very wealthy people who are not concerned about possessions, and others who very much are! We need to adopt a balance in life, unlike the businessman and the rich fool depicted in scripture, and be content with what we have, using our ability to its full potential. Winning the lottery is not the picture of biblical stewardship, and our willingness to believe that most lottery winners end up bankrupt in a few years—suggests we instinctively know that money alone is not the answer to life.[96]

Paul wrote to the Philippian church and warned them about wealth and riches:

> I have learned to be content whatever the circumstances. I know what it is to be in need, and I know what it is to have plenty. I have learned the secret of being content in any and every situation, whether well fed

---

[96] This claim has been widely attributed to the National Endowment for Financial Education, which has now retracted it. See "Research Statistic on Financial Windfalls and Bankruptcy," NEFE, January 12, 2018, www.nefe.org/news/2018/01/research-statistic-on-financial-windfalls-and-bankruptcy.aspx.

or hungry, whether living in plenty, or in want. I can do everything through him who gives me strength.[97]

What a great spiritual attitude to obtain.

The little prince told the businessman candidly that his attitude was of no consequence to the stars. In that moment, did the businessman realize that after fifty-four years, the way he conducted himself was an exercise in futility, and he had no wealth at all? Maybe some of us are just like the businessman the little prince encountered.

[97] Philippians 4:11–13 NIV.

Chapter 14

The Lamplighter

*You are the light of the world. A city on a hill cannot be hidden.
Neither do people light a lamp and put in under a bowl.
Instead they put it on a stand and it gives light to everyone in the house.
In the same way, let your light shine before men, that they may see
your good deeds and praise your Father in heaven.*
Matthew 5:14–16 (NIV)

The fifth planet that the little prince visits is a very small planet and maybe the smallest of them all. The planet has a curious inhabitant called the lamplighter. The little prince does not understand why the planet has only a lantern on it, nor for that matter why the man called the lamplighter continually and habitually lights the lamp then extinguishes it. He seems to do this around the clock, and on his planet a day goes by every minute—the planet is so small it rotates completely in a minute.

The little prince notices the lamplighter is a very diligent workman. He questions the lamplighter on why he lights the lantern, extinguishes it, then relights it and extinguishes it again. The lamplighter replies, "Because of the orders."

"What orders?" the little prince asks. The lamplighter doesn't disclose where the orders come from.

The lamplighter was a very hard worker, unlike the inhabitants of the other planets who were doing nothing of consequence, and the little prince respected and appreciated that. The lamplighter was very industrious and faithful in his work, just as the little prince had cared for his planet, the rose, the volcanoes, and the removal of the baobab trees. The lamplighter had what appears to be good stewardship principles, and he followed the orders or directives that have been given to him.

This is similar to the directives or orders that God gave to humanity: "Whatever your hand finds to do, do it with all your might, for in the grave where you are going there is neither working nor planning nor knowledge nor wisdom."[98] This is the course for humanity since the fall in the Garden of Eden and original sin.[99] The Bible says,

> Because you have listened to the voice of your own wife and you have eaten from its tree about which I commanded you saying, you shall not eat from it: curse the ground because of you; with hard labor you shall each eat from it all the days of your life.[100]

The lamplighter was condemned to a life of continual toil and labor without any rest or sleep. Such was his lot in life. But the little prince respected the lamplighter in that he was actually doing something for someone else, putting others before his own well-being.

Why would the lamp or lantern be so important to light the planet continuously? Night came every thirty seconds. Maybe light represented God or the entity that the lamplighter was working so hard for. Maybe that's the person or thing that gave the orders. While we do not know, we do know God is light.[101] One never knows where the orders originated, but the lamplighter was faithful to his orders.

The lamplighter's job is very important to him. The little prince

---

[98] Ecclesiastes 10:9 NIV.
[99] "Original sin" is the sin attributed to Adam that was transferred to all of humanity for disobeying God's directives by eating the forbidden fruit. Man is now relegated to a life of hard labor and toil.
[100] Genesis 3:17 NASB.
[101] John 1:5 NIV.

thought that he would or could be friends with the lamplighter because of his diligence, but the planet was too small for both of them to live. But certainly the little prince took notice of the good works of the lamplighter. If the lamplighter had not been obedient to his orders, the little prince would not have been able to discern and view the diligence of the lamplighter.

Chapter 15

A Good-for-Nothing Geographer

*For if you possess these qualities in increasing measure,
they will keep you from being ineffective and unproductive
in your knowledge our Lord Jesus Christ.*
2 Peter 1:8 (NIV)

The next planet the little prince visits is very large—much larger than the previous planet with the lamplighter he had just left. On this planet lived an old man who wrote a lot of books. He was a geographer. Geographers study the Earth or planet and the attributes of its land, features, and inhabitants. The little prince did not know what a geographer was until it was explained to him. *Finally*, the little prince thought, *here is someone on these planets who has a real profession*! The little prince was initially excited to meet a person of substance but quickly faced disappointment.

The little prince thought that the planet was the most beautiful he had ever seen. He inquired of the geographer whether the planet had oceans and mountains. The geographer responded that he didn't know! The little prince thought this peculiar, in that the geographer had just explained to him that his job was to document the topography of a given area, which would include oceans, rivers, and mountains. The little prince wondered why the geographer would not know the features of the planet he lived on. To the little prince, this was foolishness.

I am again reminded of how Jesus would instruct his followers through parables, which are spiritual examples giving insight into the kingdom of heaven. The question that appears to have occurred to the little prince by observation of the geographer is, was he doing anything of consequence? Much like the parable Jesus taught of the wise and foolish builders who were building a house on different foundations, a person would be considered a wise builder if he prepared and worked for the future: "When the rain came down, the streams rose, and the winds blew and beat against the house; yet it did not fall."[102] Jesus said that those who rejected his teachings and words were building their homes on sand and were foolish because the house will not survive.

Compare the foolish attitude of the geographer. It was very peculiar that he was a geographer who lived on a beautiful planet but never got out of his chair to explore it. The geographer mistakenly believed that was the job of the explorer, which did not even exist on his planet! This so-called geographer was ill-prepared for any natural disaster that might occur on his planet. What if the planet had dangerous baobab trees that if unchecked would destroy this beautiful planet? Or what if a volcano erupted, or there was a massive earthquake? The geographer was unaware of the oceans, rivers, and natural resources that could dramatically impact the planet and his daily living, all unbeknownst to the geographer, who did not know what existed on his own beautiful planet.

The next issue that the geographer raises is mortality and immortality, a subject that becomes very important to the little prince. In this discussion, the little prince could not understand why the geographer did not record any flowers in his books. The little prince protests that on his planet, his rose is the most important thing. But the geographer said that because flowers are ephemeral, meaning temporary, they are not recorded in geography books. When the little prince learned of the mortality of the flower, he experienced regret for leaving the rose.

---

[102] Matthew 7:24–25 NIV.

Humans, too, are much like the little prince's rose; we are ephemeral, lasting only a short time, here today and gone tomorrow. Saint Paul talked about the tent we call the earthly body and its transitory nature through the metaphor of the tent:

> One day we will be transformed to an immortal for our heavenly dwelling. For while we are in this tent we grow in this burden we do not wish to be unclothed but to be clothed with our heavenly dwelling so that what is mortal may be swallowed up by life.[103]

The little prince is perplexed that the geographer hasn't enjoyed the simple things of nature right on the planet that he lived. Although the geographer explains what things are temporal, he does not take that into account in his own life and enjoy the beauty of life. Do we do the same in failing to perceive the time in which we live and to appreciate the simple things of life? The fitness footwear company Reebok had a slogan: "Life is short. Play hard." I'm not sure I fully agree with that as a saying, but I think we must appreciate the time we have in life and do the best we can to please God.

After his exchange with the geographer, who wasn't much of a geographer at all, being too lazy even to explore his own planet, the little prince asked what planet he should go to next. The geographer replied, "You should go to Earth." The little prince willingly accepts this advice and is soon on his way to Earth. Now the journey begins!

---

[103] 2 Corinthians 5:4 NIV.

Chapter 16

The Earth

*The Earth is the Lord's, and everything in it,
the world, and all who live in it.*
Psalm 24:1 (NIV)

It is evident from scripture that God created the heavens, which would include all planets and Earth, as well as all the creatures the little prince has so far encountered. In Genesis, the first book of the Bible, Moses recounts how everything was formed. God creates something out of nothing:

> In the beginning God created the heaven and the earth. And the earth was without form, and void; and darkness was upon the face of the deep. And the spirit of God moved upon the face of the waters.[104]

This creation of something from nothing is said to be ex nihilo, Latin for "out of nothingness."[105]

The description of Earth by the little prince is somewhat vague,

---

[104] Genesis 1:1–2 KJV.
[105] *Creatio ex nihilo* is the creation out of nothing and not out of some substance pre-existing itself. See "Creatio Ex Nihilo," Encyclopedia.com, https://www.encyclopedia.com/education/encyclopedias-almanacs-transcripts-and-maps/creatio-ex-nihilo, accessed November 27, 2023.

but I think that based on the planets he had visited before—those of the king, the geographer, the businessman, the lamplighter, the tippler, and the conceited man—certainly the Earth comprises more than what the little prince has experienced before.

What experiences are in store for the little prince on this planet called Earth? Maybe the little prince will experience the joys of life, friendship, and happiness rather than what he dealt with on his own planet with his rose and the baobab trees. As I approach this chapter, I hope that the little prince encounters more here on Earth than the lamplighter or the tippler.

The Bible says that each day has its own troubles: "Therefore do not be anxious about tomorrow, for tomorrow will be anxious for itself. Sufficient for the day is its own trouble."[106] So whatever of life's circumstances the little prince will face as he explores this new planet called Earth, the Bible promises us that through any and all of life's circumstances or troubles, God will always be present to comfort and to lead us. This is true whether the times are good or troubled. Certainly one must also keep an eye on the afterlife. The prophet Isaiah wrote, "For behold, I will create new heavens and a new earth. The former things will not be remembered, nor will they come to mind."[107]

Biblically, Earth is the planet that God chose to have life and inhabitants on. It is curious that the other planets the little prince visited had few inhabitants, or seemingly only one, and that nothing of substance was going on. According to NASA, "the earth is the only place we know of so far that's inhabited by living things. It's also the only planet in our solar system with liquid water on the surface."[108]

Is the earth special and specifically selected for the little prince to experience the emotions and circumstances of life? We shall see in his travels and encounters on this big blue marble.

---

[106] Matthew 6:34 Bahrain Literal Bible.
[107] Isaiah 65:17.
[108] "Earth," NASA Solar System Explorations, https://science.nasa.gov/earth/facts, accessed November 27, 2023.

Chapter 17

The Snake

So the Lord God said to the serpent, because you have done this, cursed are you above all livestock and all wild animals! You will crawl on your belly and you will eat dust all the days of your life.
Genesis 3:14 (ESV)

The little prince's first encounter on Earth is not what he expected. He thought he was going to meet people, but instead he encounters a snake. A snake has negative connotations biblically and socially, as most people dislike or fear snakes. We know that early in the Bible, the devil took the form of a snake to tempt Adam and Eve. For that deception, the snake apparently was cursed by God, and having lost its legs was therefore cursed to crawl and be trampled on the ground. There was also a prophecy related to the deception of the snake that represented the devil, to the effect that "it shall bruise thy heel and thou shall crush its head."[109] This references theologically how the Messiah, the Christ, would overcome and crush sin and death brought on by the devil in the form of a snake.

The snake throughout scripture mostly stands for the proposition of harm and danger, temptation and sin, and of course the devil. But there is an instance in the Old Testament when the snake is depicted as good and helpful and life-giving. When Moses delivered

---

[109] Genesis 3:15 KJV.

the Israelites out of captivity from the Egyptians, they ended up in a barren desert. The Israelites complained that they wished they were back in captivity, where they had shelter and food. The Lord was very angry at these constant complaints and was disappointed with the people of Israel, because he had directed Moses to free them from captivity in answer to their own prayerful requests. Therefore the Lord set upon the Israelites venomous snakes to execute judgment against them for unbelief and disobedience. Many of the Israelites died from the bites inflicted by the snakes.

Eventually, the Israelites realized their sin and rebellion against God in complaining about Moses, and repented: "We have sinned for we have spoken against the Lord and against thee; pray unto the Lord, that he take away the serpents from us." The Lord then fashioned a cure for them: "The Lord said to Moses make thee a fiery serpent and sit it upon a pole and it shall come to pass, that everyone that is bitten when he looks upon it shall live."[110]

Snakes do not always represent the devil or death. In this situation, the serpent represented life and healing, and that may be why the American Medical Association has adopted Moses' serpent on the staff as its emblem.[111]

Following our initial impressions, we will discover in *The Little Prince* whether the snake represents something nefarious, good, or maybe both. It is curious that the first creature that the little prince came in contact with on Earth was a snake. One of the first encounters recorded in the Bible is humanity's encounter with the snake in the Garden of Eden. We know, too, that Jesus was tempted in the wilderness, much like a desert, where he met the devil (the snake) and was tempted by him.

Immediately after Jesus was baptized by John the Baptist, the Bible records that "heaven was opened, and they saw the spirit of God descending like a dove and alighting on him and a voice from

---

[110] Numbers 21:7–8 KJV.
[111] The AMA symbol dates back to antiquity and represents the serpent-entwined staff as it appeared in the book of Exodus as a point of healing for those that looked upon it.

heaven said, "This is my son whom I love with him I am well-pleased."[112] Jesus then was taken alone and isolated out in the desert, without food for forty days. After the period of his fasting ended, the tempter came, and confronted and tested Jesus to sin on three separate occasions. The following verses unmask the identity of the tempter as Satan.

The little prince, much like Jesus experienced temptation by the devil, is confronted with a snake. Are we to think of the little prince as experiencing his own hour of temptation or trial by the devilish snake in the desert?

In the temptation of Christ, Satan had so much authority and power that he was able to take Jesus to a very high mountain and show him all the kingdoms of the world in their splendor. " 'All this I will give to you,' he said, 'if you will bow down and worship me,' " echoed by what the snake said to the little prince: "I am more powerful than the finger of a king." When the little prince doubted the power of the snake because it was "no thicker than a finger," the snake said, "I can carry you further than any ship could take you. I have the power to send you back to where you came. And then he said to the little prince that he was very weak, and when he grows homesick and wants to return to the planet he came from the snake could send him there."[113]

Would the little prince remember the things the snake proposed and allow him to take him there? What does this all mean? Is it the beginning of the end for the little prince and his encounter with the snake? We will see how this ends.

---

[112] John 3:16–17 NIV.
[113] Saint-Exupéry, *The Little Prince*, p. 92.

Chapter 18

One Flower, Three Petals

Go ye therefore and teach all nations, baptizing them in the name of the Father, and of the Son and of the Holy Spirit.
Matthew 28:19 (KJV)

During the little prince's travels on this new planet called Earth, he encounters a flower. It is an unnamed flower, but it has three petals. It is not like his rose. This flower with three petals is not much of anything, and the encounter is very brief. The little prince asks the flower if it had seen any men. The flower responds only once but says something very interesting about the temporal existence of a man compared to a flower: "they have no roots and the wind blows them away."[114]

The Bible teaches the same principal espoused by the flower with three petals. "As for man, his days are like grass. As a flower of the field so flourishes. When the wind has panned over it, it is no more and its place acknowledged it no longer."[115]

The flower didn't think much of man in that they have no roots and consequently are blown by the wind of circumstance. But it was an interesting observation as it relates to humanity made by the flower. And why one flower, three petals? Why not one flower with

---
[114] Saint-Exupéry, *The Little Prince*, p. 95.
[115] Psalm 103:15 NIV.

multiple petals, or several flowers with multiple petals? What did the one flower with three petals represent?

The little prince encountered a flower of unknown origin that had only three petals and no thorns. One flower, three petals. Could this signify the triune God? One God, three persons. Historically, the universal Christian church has relied and accepted the doctrine of the triune God, similar to one flower three petals. This chapter, though the shortest in *The Little Prince*, may contain the most Christology and theology, coming from the flower—one flower, three petals.

The Trinity is one of the most mysterious of all Christian doctrines.[116] Some argue that the Trinity is not mentioned in the Bible, but there are several references to the Father, Son, and the Holy Spirit acting in conjunction as one. In the scripture that serves as the epigraph to the current chapter, Jesus directs the apostles to proclaim the good news to all people in the name of the Father, the Son, and the Holy Spirit. The book of Galatians supports the triune theology: "He is the image of the invisible God, the first born over all creation … for God was pleased to have his fullness dwell in him."[117]

Referencing the second person of the Trinity, the Son or Word, the Lord Jesus Christ, John's gospel echoes similar concepts of a Trinitarian view of God: One God, three persons: "In the beginning was the Word and the Word was with God, and the Word was God."[118] In later verses of scripture, the Word is uncloaked to be Jesus

---

[116] "A Trinity doctrine is commonly expressed as the statement that that one God exists as or in three equally divine 'Persons', the Father, the Son, and the Holy Spirit. Every term in this statement (God, exists, as or in, equally divine, Person) has been variously misunderstood. The guiding principle has been the creedal declaration that the Father, Son, and Holy Spirit of the New Testament are consubstantial (i.e. the same in substance or essence, Greek: *homoousios*). Because this shared substance or essence is a divine one, this is understood to imply that all three named individuals are divine, and equally so. Yet the three in some sense 'are' the one God of the Bible": Stanford Encyclopedia of Philosophy, s.v. "Trinity," last revised November 20, 2020, https://plato.stanford.edu/entries/trinity, accessed November 27, 2023.
[117] Galatians 1:15, 19
[118] John 1:1 NIV.

Christ. Further support for the doctrine of the triune God was vividly identified in the baptism of Jesus. John the Baptist was baptizing people in the Jordan River, and Jesus went to John to be baptized. At first John, knowing who and what Jesus was, was apprehensive about baptizing Jesus. He thought it would be more appropriate for Jesus to baptize him rather than the other way around. Jesus then told John to do what was proper, so John then baptized Jesus.

At that moment when Jesus was baptized and came out of the water, the Trinity is identified:

> At that moment heaven was opened, and he saw the Spirit of God descending like a dove, and lighting on him. And a voice from heaven said, "This is my Son, whom I love; with him I am well pleased."[119]

The "one flower, three petals" theology is revealed in this biblical event as one God, three persons: Father, Son, and Holy Spirit. The Son Jesus is being baptized, the Holy Spirit descends on him during his baptism as a dove, and the voice from heaven, which is the Father, confirms Jesus's identity as the Son. The scripture identifies the Trinity in action.

In addition to the numerous scriptural references to the doctrine of the Trinity, many creeds from the early church developed and explained the concept of the one God, three persons—the one flower, three petals. The Nicene Creed, adopted in AD 325, states, "And I believe in the Holy Spirit the Lord and the giver of life, who proceeds from the Father and the Son together is worshipped and glorified." The Belgic Confession, article 8, states:

> In keeping with this truth and the Word of God we believe in One God who is one single essence, in whom there are three persons, really, truly, eternally distinct according to their incommunicable properties-Father, Son and Holy Spirit.

---

[119] Matthew 3:16–17 NIV.

Article 1 of the Church of England 1521 states:

> There is but one living and one true God everlasting, without body, parts, or passions of intimate power, wisdom and goodness; the maker and preserver of all things both visible and invisible. And in unity of this Godhead there be three persons; of one substance, power and eternity; the Father, the Son and the Holy Ghost.

What may be the reasons Saint-Exupéry chose to have the little prince interact with one flower, three petals? This may signify his intent to interact with the theology of the triune God.

Chapter 19

All Alone

But he would withdraw to desolate places and pray...
Luke 5:16 (ESV)

Once again the little prince is isolated and all alone in his travels. In his journey on Earth, he comes to a place that appears to be desolate, filled only with mountains, deserted with no people. He calls out "Good morning!" and he hears the same back as an echo. He believes that the inhabitants of Earth, the men he is looking for, are responding to him. The little prince never experienced the phenomenon known as an echo in a canyon or mountain range. As we know, he only had three small volcanoes on his planet, possibly asteroid B-612, which was very small.

When the little prince called out in the mountain range and heard his echo in return, he concluded that the inhabitants had no imagination, much like grown-ups, because they only repeated back to him exactly what he had said. Although the little prince was looking for people on this planet called Earth and was all alone, he wasn't scared or lonely. He didn't act very concerned about his predicament, or maybe it wasn't any predicament at all. It appears the little prince found comfort when he was alone. Like the little prince, are we really ever alone?

The Bible teaches, "It is the Lord who goes before you. He will be with you; he will not leave you or forsake you. Do not fear or be dismayed."[120] In the past the little prince was distraught about the rose and the way she treated him, but the Bible promises, "the Lord is near the broken-hearted and saves the crushed in spirit."[121]

Even Jesus withdrew himself and was alone when he would pray. There are several critical instances in the life of Jesus when he went to be alone and to pray. Before Jesus performed the miracle of walking on water, he withdrew from the disciples and went to a solitary place in the mountains to pray.[122] Before Jesus chose the disciples, he went to the mountainside alone to pray.[123] In the Transfiguration,[124] as Jesus was praying the appearance of his face underwent a dramatic change, and his clothes became bright as a flash of lightning. Two prophets, Moses and Elijah, appeared in glorious splendor, talking with Jesus.[125]

These important events occurred when Jesus isolated himself from the distractions of the world, to pray and have fellowship with God. Jesus continually went away from people to be alone, but he was never really alone—he was with God the Father. And ultimately, Jesus went to a solitary place called the Garden of Gethsemane to pray before his crucifixion and death. He looked for solace and peace with God to overcome the circumstances and confusion of the world.

Being alone was important for the little prince, as it was for Jesus. Today, people are often afraid to be alone and to face themselves for who and what they are. In the story of the little prince, we see that he often disappears by himself. It does not appear that the little prince was upset at being alone; in fact, he rather enjoyed it. He reluctantly left his planet and traveled to unknown worlds, making numerous stops until he arrived at Earth. What else will this lone explorer experience in his travels?

---

[120] Deuteronomy 31:8 ESV.
[121] Psalm 34:18 ESV.
[122] Mark 6:46 NIV.
[123] Luke 6:12 NIV.
[124] The transfiguration is an uncloaking of the majesty and divinity of Jesus Christ, both before the incarnation and after his ascension. It discloses Jesus as both God and Man to the disciples.
[125] Luke 9:29–31 NIV.

Chapter 20

The Beloved

Now there was leaning on Jesus' bosom one of his disciples, whom Jesus loved.
John 13:23 (KJV)

In his journey on Earth, the little prince, to his surprise, encounters 5,000 roses, seemingly just like his rose on his home planet, possibly asteroid B-612. This discovery is somewhat of a shock to the little prince because he was under the impression that his rose was the only rose like it anywhere. When the little prince saw 5,000 of these roses that appeared similar to his rose, he was saddened and thought that his rose would be very upset to learn about the other roses. This is a dramatic realization to the little prince; because he thought his rose was the only one and special, he considered himself rich because of the value of his particular rose. He now realizes that she may be a common rose, and with that he becomes so upset that he cries over this newfound information.

This chapter raises the issue of the uniqueness of his rose. Was she unique and special, or just like every other common rose? In this light, I am prompted to wonder whether Jesus had any special people in his life. I thought Jesus had no favorites, but loves everybody the same and equally. Is it possible for Jesus to have some who were closer to him, and yet still love and care for all? The Bible teaches, "Jesus loves us all, and died so all would be saved."[126]

If we look to scripture, we find that Jesus did a great miracle for all when he fed 5,000 people with the five loaves of bread and two fish.[127] Jesus took the loaves and fish, gave thanks to God, and broke the loaves; the disciples then gave them to the people to eat. Jesus did this miracle for the benefit of those who had come to hear him preach in a remote place, when he knew that evening was approaching and many might not be able to eat for some time. Jesus cared for the well-being of 5,000 people he did not know. He certainly did not know them as intimately as he did the other twelve disciples.

Even among the people and the disciples around him, Jesus favored some more than others. Some disciples were unique or special to Jesus. He said John the Baptist was greatest of all men: "I tell you the truth, among those born of women there has not risen anyone greater than John the Baptist."[128] Clearly John the Baptist was a person like the 5,000 people Jesus fed, but John was special to Jesus and different from the 5,000. Among the disciples, there were the special twelve who were selected by Jesus—less Judas, who betrayed Jesus, but with eleven remaining. Yet the Apostle John was called the "beloved disciple," the one Jesus loved. In John's own gospel, he refers to himself as the disciple Jesus loved, as disclosed when he recorded what occurred on the very first Easter morning. On the first day of the week, which was Sunday, three days after the crucifixion, Peter and "the other disciple, the one Jesus loved"—that is, John the gospeler—were told that the tomb where Jesus was buried was empty: "They have taken the Lord out of the tomb, and we don't know where they have put him." Peter and the other disciple ran for the tomb, but "the other disciple" that Jesus loved—John the beloved—outran Peter and arrived first.[129]

Peter and John, along with (unfortunately) Judas Iscariot, are

---

[126] John 4:9–11 NIV.
[127] Matthew 14:17 NIV.
[128] Matthew 11:11 NIV.
[129] John 20:1–4 NIV.

perhaps the best known of the twelve apostles. John and his brother James were with Peter at some of the most significant moments of Jesus' earthly ministry. John is more personally close to Jesus than the other disciples. John the Apostle was there for the Transfiguration of Jesus, along with Peter and James, where they saw Jesus transfigured, foreshadowing his resurrected body, which was to come. What may be even more important to demonstrate John's uniqueness to Jesus is not only that he was known as the "beloved disciple" but that as Jesus hung on the cross near death, some of his last words were to John.

> When Jesus saw his mother there, and the disciple whom he loved [John] standing nearby, he said to his mother, "Dear woman, here is your son, and to the disciple, "Here is your mother. From that time on this disciple [John] took her into his house.[130]

This shows what a special relationship Jesus had with John, unique from that of the other disciples.

The little prince's rose may be like John the Apostle. Although the eleven other disciples and the 5,000 people Jesus fed were loved, they were not special and unique to Jesus. And although there may have been 5,000 other roses, the little prince's rose was unique for him and loved, making her the only rose in the world to him.

---

[130] John 19:26–27 NIV.

Chapter 21

The Fox

One who has unreliable friends soon come to ruin, but there is a friend who sticks closer than a brother.
Proverbs 18:24 (NIV)

One of the longest chapters in *The Little Prince* is when the little prince meets the fox, who would eventually become his dear loving friend. It is striking to me that the little prince saw the fox under an apple tree. As legend has it, the fruit that Eve pulled from the tree of knowledge of good and evil may have been an apple. That may or may not be true, but the apple has been associated with the fall of humanity as the biblical narrative describes in the Garden of Eden:

> And when the woman saw that tree was good for food and it was pleasant to the eyes, and the tree desired to make one wise, she took of the fruit thereof, and did eat, and gave it unto her husband with her, and he did eat it.[131]

So is it happenstance that the little prince first meets the fox under an apple tree? There may be a relation of wisdom and knowledge between the apple tree and the fox.

---

[131] Genesis 3:6 KJV.

In the Song of Solomon, we have already discerned that the writer describes a romantic relationship between two lovers in terms of a rose, a lily among thorns, and an apple among trees:

> I am the Rose of Sharon, and the Lily of the Valley.
> As a lily among thorns, is in my love among daughter.
> As the apple tree among the trees of the wood.[132]

In meeting the fox, the little prince tells of his own condition. The little prince was very sad and wanted to play with the fox—or someone, for that matter. But the fox said, "Since I am untamed, I could not oblige."

The little prince questioned the fox about what "untamed" meant. The fox initially did not answer the questions of the little prince and instead asked the little prince why he was there. The little prince said that he was looking for man. Man being the archenemy of the fox, the fox was concerned because men hunt foxes, and the little prince might be hunting him.

Foxes are referenced often in scripture and not in a very positive light—usually for their sly and cunning disposition. The fox could also stand for the proposition of destruction, as in the Old Testament story of Sampson. When Sampson found out his that wife had cheated on him with a Philistine, he retaliated in a very peculiar way. He caught three hundred foxes, tied them together in pairs by their tails, and attached a firebrand to their two tied tails. He set the brands on fire and let the foxes loose to run blazing into the standing fields of the Philistines. The stalks and the standing corn burnt up along with their vineyards and olives, causing immense destruction.[133]

As we have seen, the author of *The Little Prince* references numerous biblical themes throughout his story. The Song of Solomon (2:15 KJV) makes another reference to the destructive capacity of the fox: "Take us the little foxes that spoil the vines for our vines

---

[132] Song of Solomon 2:1–3 KJV.
[133] Judges 15:4–6 KJV.

have tender grapes." In his commentary on the Song of Solomon, Matthew Henry writes of

> the little foxes, that creep insensibly; for, though they are little, they do great mischief, they spoil the vines, which they must by no means be suffered to do at any time, especially now when our vines have tender grapes that must be preserved, or the vintage will fail. Believers are as vines, weak but useful plants; their fruits are as tender crops at first, which must have time to come to maturity. … Seize the little foxes, the first risings of sin, the little ones of Babylon those sins that seem little, for they often prove very dangerous.[134]

The fox revisits a topic that has been discussed before with the little prince, the issue of uniqueness and friendship. The little prince discloses that he is looking for a friend. The fox tells the little prince that he is no different from 100,000 other little boys. The little prince is perplexed by this. Is this the same issue as when he learned that his rose, which he thought was unique, was like the other 5,000 other roses that the little prince encountered?

The fox explained that if the little prince spent time and energy taming him, then the relationship would change. The fox would become unique and special to the little prince, and the little prince would be special and unique to the fox, not like the 100,000 other little boys. The little prince began to understand the concept of friendship, uniqueness, and taming. He was able to contemplate the possibility that the rose had tamed him, or maybe he had tamed the rose, much as the fox wanted the little prince to tame him so they would need and care for each other.

The fox was intrigued by this creature and thought the little

---

[134] Matthew Henry, commentary on the Song of Solomon, as cited by "Biblical Foxes," Christianity 201 (July 28, 2013), https://christianity201.wordpress.com/2013/07/28/biblical-foxes, accessed November 27, 2023.

prince's hair was so beautiful and golden that it matched the color of the beautiful grain fields of gold! The one apprehension the fox had toward the little prince is that he considered him somewhat of a little man, and men were feared by the fox because they hunt and kill foxes. When the fox heard footsteps in the woods, he feared that it was one of those men hunting him. The fox thought, though, that if the little prince spent the necessary time, the same time each day, the fox would be able to discern the sound of the little prince's footsteps from that of the hunters'. It would make the fox very happy to have a friend. The fox desperately wanted a friend, and so did the little prince.

Although the little prince's time was limited on Earth, he embarked on this endeavor to tame the fox. The fox then dispenses wisdom to the little prince, saying that men don't appreciate friendship and are only concerned about what they can have or what they can buy. This concept of want and need is expressed in the teachings of Christ:

> Therefore I tell you do not worry about your life, what you will eat or drink or about your body, or what you will wear. Is life not more important than food, and the body more important than clothes?[135]

Jesus cautioned humanity on these perils, and similar wisdom dispensed by the fox echoes: "Watch out! Be on guard against all kinds of greed; a man's life does not consist in the abundance of his possessions."[136]

The fox tells the little prince that he needs patience in the process of taming. Taming takes time, effort, much like discipline, and discipleship in scripture. Jesus indicates that there is a cost associated with following him. When Jesus was confronted with someone who requested that Jesus make him a follower, much like the fox wanting to be tamed by the little prince, Jesus cautioned him that "foxes have

---

[135] Matthew 6:25 NIV.
[136] Luke 12:15 NIV.

holes and birds of the air have nests, but the Son of Man has no place to lay his head."[137]

Eventually the taming of the fox was accomplished by the little prince. Although the little prince had told the fox that his time on Earth was limited and he would have to leave eventually, when the time came it was very upsetting to the fox. The fox had grown very fond of the little creature, but the little prince had thought that this taming was a useless exercise, since he had to leave. The fox reminded the little prince that the time spent taming the fox made the fox unique to the little prince, and the little prince unique to the fox! Now the little prince was not like the other 100,000 other little boys.

The fox had taught the little prince a very valuable lesson. He would now understand that although there were 5,000 other roses, they weren't his unique rose! Of the 5,000 roses, the little prince reflected that "one could not die for you"[138]—suggesting he *would* die for the sake of his unique rose. Is this an incognito reference to the life and sacrifice of Jesus? Jesus spoke to this very concept that moves the little prince: "Greater love hath no man than this, that a man lay down his life for a friend."[139] Jesus referred to his own sacrifice in saying, "For God so loved the world that he gave his only begotten Son, that whoever believes in him should not perish but have everlasting life." Amongst all the words and anecdotes of the little prince, his little gem of a statement to the rose unlocks the lofty theological concepts embedded in this masterpiece.

The little prince now understood that his rose was special and unique to him in all the world. Because he tamed the rose, or the rose tamed him, they had a special bond. The little prince cared for the rose, watered the rose, put a glass globe on the rose to keep her warm, and a screen around her so she would always be protected. The little prince made sure the rose was always comfortable and protected and not eaten or otherwise harmed. He has now learned this lesson

---

[137] Matthew 8:20 NIV.
[138] Saint-Exupéry, *The Little Prince*, p. 110.
[139] In the Christian faith *atonement* means the symbolizing death of Christ as reconciliation is made possible through faith in him.

of life and death from the fox, so very similar to what Jesus said about sacrificing his life for the life of another.

After this exchange with the fox, the little prince is ready to say goodbye to his now tamed friend, and with that the fox gave the little prince a parting gift of wisdom. This may be one of the most significant statements in all of the book titled *The Little Prince*, and what I believe to be the apex of the meanings expressed in it thus far and throughout the whole book. The fox tells the little prince this: "It is only with the heart that one can see rightly; what is essential is invisible to the naked eye."[140] This reminds me of the definition of faith in the book of Hebrews (11:1 KJV): "faith is the substance of things hoped for, the evidence of things not seen."

The little prince now understood much of what he did not know before. He realized the important things of creaturely life cannot be seen or bought but rather are of the heart. And with that, the little prince departed and left his fox.

A Note on Bible References to the Fox

Another interesting scripture that references the fox has significant eschatological[141] implications. It is found in the Old Testament book of Lamentations (5:18), where the writer is actually lamenting the condition of Israel, that they have been orphaned and are fatherless, and are under persecution and forced labor. The nation had been delivered into hands of their enemies because their forefathers sinned and they now bear their inequities. The scripture then talks about the reformation of the nation after the prophesized destruction of the two temples in Jerusalem, when Mount Zion will stand desolate and "foxes will walk upon it." The destruction of the temples has in

---

[140] Saint-Exupéry, *The Little Prince*, p. 112.
[141] In Christian theology, *eschatology* is the doctrine of last things. It is a term derived from Greek originally referring in Western religious studies to Jewish, Christian, and Muslim beliefs about the end of world history, the resurrection of the dead, and the Last Judgment.

fact already occurred, so will the prophecies by Zechariah about the temple being rebuilt now come to pass?

One event has to take place before the rebuilding of the temples: foxes must walk upon the desolate land. Has this condition now been fulfilled?

In 2019, the *Jerusalem Post* reported the response of Rabbi Shmuel Rabinowitz, rabbi of the Western Wall and Holy Site, to photos that had been taken recently showing random foxes wandering around the Temple Mount: "One cannot refrain from crying at the site of the fulfillment of the prophecy of 'foxes will walk on it.' "[142] The fox not only has important meaning to the story of *The Little Prince* but also has significant biblical ramifications for Judeo-Christians.

---

[142] "Foxes seen walking near the Western Wall, fulfilling biblical promise," *Jerusalem Post* (August 8, 2019), https://www.jpost.com/israel-news/foxes-seen-walking-near-the-western-wall-fulfilling-biblical-promise-598053, accessed November 22, 2023.

Chapter 22

The Switchman

*"This is meaningless! Meaningless!" Said the teacher,
everything is meaningless."*
Ecclesiastes 1:1 (NIV)

After the little prince leaves the company of his fox, he encounters a person who operates a railroad. That person is called a switchman. I am assuming the reason he is called the switchman is that he sorts travelers and puts them on the correct train to get to their destinations.

In this encounter, the little prince sees three trains, the first of which has extremely bright lights on it and sounds like thunder. Light has always been associated with God, and Jesus is called the "the light of the world."[143] The book of Revelation depicts a light so bright that the sun will not be needed:

> And night will be no more. They will need no light or sun, for the Lord will be their light, and they will reign forever and ever."[144]

Bright lights and thunder are frequent biblical images.
The Psalmist wrote, "the voice is upon the waters; the God of

---
[143] John 8:12 KJV.
[144] Revelation 22:5 ESV.

Glory thunders. The Lord is over many waters."[145] In Revelation, we find "out of the throne comes flashing of lightning and sounds and peals of thunder."[146] These trains are no ordinary trains.

We never learn the destination of the people on the trains. But it doesn't seem anybody was very happy, except for the children. Does this chapter contemplate the final destination of all the passengers? The Bible teaches the ultimate glory of all humanity is to be part of God's "train" that leads to the heavenly realms: "When He ascended on high, he led a train of vanquished foes as he bestowed gifts on men."[147]

The little prince saw three brightly lit trains that sounded like thunder. They were carrying passengers, but no one knows where they were going. Why three trains? One for heaven, one for hell, and one for purgatory? That secret lies within the province of the Jesuit-educated author of *The Little Prince*, Antoine de Saint-Exupéry. But the Psalmist wrote, "You ascended on high, leading a host of captives in your train and receiving gifts from above." Let us hope that one of the three trains led to the destination of heaven. Were only the children with childlike faith going there?

In life and death, there appear different possibilities with different destinations for eternity to the afterlife, as many believe. The little prince began to ask questions about where the trains were going. Nobody knew! He noticed two trains going in opposite directions. The little prince could not understand what was going on. The switchman gave the little prince a life lesson in response: "No one is ever satisfied where he is."[148]

In contrast to the attitudes of the train passengers, the Bible tells us that the Apostle Paul experienced divergent conditions of life, from being a well-educated, affluent man of influence and stature to being broken, beaten, thrown into prison, poor, and displaced by his own Jewish community. We are to be content in all life's

---

[145] Psalm 29:3 NSV.
[146] Revelation 4:5 NIV.
[147] Ephesians 4:9 AMPC.
[148] Saint-Exupéry, *The Little Prince*, p. 114.

circumstances, which include both the good and trouble. Paul wrote, "I am not saying this because I am in need, for I have learned to be content whatever the circumstances."[149] Job expresses the same belief: "What? Shall we receive good at the hands of God, and shall we not receive evil?"[150]

In the famous poem "The Road Not Taken," Robert Frost wrote of the "two roads [that] diverged in a yellow wood" and his regret that "I could not travel both":

> Two roads diverged in a wood, and I—
> I took the one less traveled by,
> And that has made all the difference.

For me, these words of wisdom echo those of Jesus on the two paths of life:

> Enter through the narrow gate, for wide is the gate and broad is the road that leads to destruction and many enter through it, but small is the gate and narrow is the road that leads to life and few find it."[151]

Was the destination of one of the trains eternal life?

---

[149] Philippians 4:11 NIV.
[150] Job 3:10 KJV.
[151] Matthew 7:13–14 NIV.

Chapter 23

The Merchant

Sir, give me this water so I that I won't get thirsty and have to keep coming here to draw water.
John 4:15 (NIV)

The little prince now encounters a merchant, who is selling a very odd product. The product he is selling is a pill that, evidently, quenches your thirst so you never get thirsty or have to drink water again. All you need to do is take one pill each week, and you won't need anything to drink.

The little prince inquired why these pills were necessary. The merchant said that by taking one pill a week, you can save 53 minutes of time. If you multiply 53 minutes each week by 52 weeks, that equates to 2,756 minutes or about 45 hours a year—about two days of time saved. The merchant does not tell the little prince how the time saved is calculated; maybe it's the amount of time spent drinking or hydrating, or for that matter going to the bathroom!

In any case, would the taking of these pills actually be beneficial? In fact, to point out the frugality of this invention, the little prince told the merchant that if he took the pill and had the extra 53 minutes every week, he would like to take a walk to a fresh spring. Why would you take a walk to a fresh spring if you don't need to drink water?

Might this pill be suggestive of the living water Jesus refers to in the Bible? It is a perplexing thought as to why Saint-Exupéry would include this in *The Little Prince*. Scripture may give us insight into this pill that quenches one's thirst without the need to drink any physical water again. We have already mentioned one of the times that quenching your thirst is referenced in the Bible, and not in a positive way—the parable Jesus taught about the rich man and Lazarus. But here it appears that the author of *The Little Prince* chose to have the merchant selling this special pill that has the ability to quench one's thirst indefinitely. Is this suggestive of the afterlife or living water that Jesus referred to in his exchange with the woman at the well?

In John's gospel, Jesus meets a Samaritan woman at Jacob's well. Jesus is thirsty and asks the woman for a drink. The Samaritan woman is perplexed because she recognizes Jesus as a Jew, and the religious Jews would have nothing to do with the hated Samaritans. When the woman states that she didn't believe Jews would associate with Samaritans, Jesus replied, "if you knew the gift of God and who it is that asks you for a drink you would have asked him for living waters."[152]

Jesus then explained to the woman that the living water he was talking about is spiritual, not physical water one would drink. Jesus proclaimed,

> Everyone who drinks this water will be thirsty again, but whoever drinks the water I give him will never thirst. Indeed the water I give him will become in him a spring welling up to eternal life.[153]

Is the living water of eternal life what the merchant was trying to sell in the pill? A pill so that you would never need to drink or be thirsty again? That water can only be provided by Jesus. Is Jesus the merchant incognito?

---

[152] John 4:10 NIV.
[153] John 4:13 NIV.

Chapter 24

The Pilot

I have no one else like him who will show genuine concern for your welfare.
Philippians 2:20 (NIV)

The pilot is now reintroduced into the story of *The Little Prince*. We have not had any interaction between the little prince and the pilot in some time. The little prince was on his own adventures as he would appear and disappear in the eight days since the pilot had crashed his plane in the Sahara desert.

The little prince begins to tell the pilot the story of the merchant. The story probably came at an inopportune time, because at that point, the pilot had not been able to fix his airplane, and he is running out of water. The pilot must have thought, *What an odd story to tell me!* His little friend had once met a merchant who sold a pill that could take away your thirst, so that you would never again need to drink any water. And he told this story as the pilot was beginning to die of thirst.

The pilot relayed to the little prince the predicament of having no water. The pilot stated that it was a dire problem. After a discussion, they decided to venture out of the area where the plane had crashed to look for water. As they walked several miles together looking for water, even in this situation the pilot was able to appreciate the beauty and tranquility of the desert, even in its unforgiving harshness. As they searched for water, the pilot made an analogy between the desert and his childhood home. He recalls a legend that treasure was buried on the grounds of his house. No one ever really tried to look for it, he said, but the story gave a mystical aspect to the house. Why this story about buried treasure at his house? Maybe he is remembering his childhood or contemplating a tragic outcome or the possible death he may experience because he has not been able to find a source of water or repair his plane.

At this point in *The Little Prince*, the first suggestion of death is integrated into the story. In talking about friends, the little prince states, oddly enough, "It is a good thing to have a friend even if one is about to die."[154] Was the little prince referencing himself or the pilot? It appears that the little prince was familiar with what death is and was unfazed by it. Why would a little child understand death? What was the little prince thinking at that point in time? He had built a friendship with the pilot over these last eight days, and was he thinking that the pilot was near death? It was now important for the little prince to have friendships, even if that friendship didn't last very long.

Did the little prince learn that from the fox? This is one of the most intriguing statements the little prince has made thus far. Does this statement suggest that the little prince understands the meaning of life and death and the afterlife with living water? Living, loving, having friendships, and appreciating them for what they are? In the little prince's mind, it would be foolish not to have friends just because the friendship would be short or the friend was going to die someday, but wise to have friends in spite of death or separation, like the fox and the rose.

The little prince then became tired and fell asleep in the arms of the pilot. What a beautiful picture de Saint-Exupéry now paints: the loving pilot holding the little prince in his arms, like a father lovingly holding his child or a shepherd holding his sheep. In John 10:11 (KJV), Jesus declares, "I am the good shepherd: the good shepherd

---

[154] Saint–Exupéry, *The Little Prince*, p. 118.

giveth his life for his sheep." The little prince was sound asleep in the pilot's arms, and the pilot came to the conclusion that the creature he held in his arms was only a shell or tent, not the essence of the person. Did the pilot know that the little prince was not long for this world? The pilot echoed words used by the Apostle Paul.

> Our bodies are like tents, that we live in here on Earth. But when these tents are destroyed we know the God will again give each of us a place to live. These homes will not be buildings someone has made, but they are in heaven and will last forever.[155]

Did the author of *The Little Prince* purposely use the word "tent" to allude to this concept?

The little prince was not concerned with this life or his sad existence, not even death, but he was keenly aware of his condition and existence. In this moment holding the little prince, the pilot may have realized two things: that the little prince was not long for this world, and that the most important things are not visible with the eye but only to the heart. The pilot may have begun to unlearn the things of his adulthood and to understand things as a child once again.

---

[155] 2 Corinthians 5:1 NIV.

Chapter 25

The Well

Therefore you will joyously draw water from the springs of salvation.
Isaiah 12:3 (KJV)

The little prince and the pilot miraculously find a water supply in the Sahara desert. What they found was very interesting. They found a working well that had been dug, with a rope pulley and a bucket as though it was made for a village or town, yet no one was around. There were no people and no village. It was a curious thing to find a well in the middle of the desert—or was it?

This well was much like the one referenced in Deuteronomy 6:10–11 (NASB 1995):

> Then it shall come about when the Lord your God brings you into the land which we swore to your fathers, Abraham, Isaac, and Jacob, to give you, great and splendid cities which you did not build ... and hewn cisterns which you did not dig.

They were overjoyed to have found this well that they did not dig! What they know is that it nourished them and quenched their thirst, and most likely saved the pilot's life. The little prince may or may not have been thirsty, but the pilot's condition was dire. He had already began to experience symptoms of dehydration from lack of water, and death would have only been a few days if not hours removed. The little prince seems to have known the whereabouts of this particular well that was in the middle of the Sahara desert, but how?

During their exploration to find the well, the prince mentions two things: first, that the fox may have said where it was. Second, the little prince told the pilot that when he came to Earth one year ago (this anniversary is upon them), the location of the well was close to where he first arrived.

Historically and biblically, the significance of a well is that it is life-giving. No human or animal could survive the desert without water, and neither could the pilot. The well is mentioned many times in both the Old and New Testaments as a source of life-giving sustenance. We read in the Old Testament that for 100 pieces of silver, Jacob bought a plot of ground where he pitched his tent and lived. Jacob stayed in the area of Shechem for a long period of time and dug a well to sustain life. Thousands of years later, Jesus meets and has the exchange with the woman at the well, the very same well Jacob had dug centuries earlier.[156] Now the little prince encounters a similar type of well.

Once the pilot has been hydrated and is in his right mind, the little prince inquires whether the pilot is going to keep the promise he made to him earlier. That promise, which the pilot had forgotten about till he was reminded, was to draw a muzzle for his sheep so it wouldn't eat the little prince's rose. We remember that when the little prince first encountered the pilot, the first thing he asked of the pilot was to draw a sheep. Now he was asking the pilot to complete that drawing by adding the muzzle. The pilot reluctantly said yes and goes on to do it.

But the request gave the pilot the sense that he might not see the little prince much longer. He remembered the story of the fox and what the little prince told him: "one runs the risk of weeping a little if one lets himself be tamed."[157] The pilot is beginning to understand that his time with the little prince may be coming to an end.

---

[156] "Patriarch Jacob's Well and St. Philoumenos," Early Church History, https://earlychurchhistory.org/martyrs/jacobs-well-st-philoumenous, accessed November 27, 2023.

[157] Saint–Exupéry, *The Little Prince*, p. 128.

Chapter 26

The Snake

Listen, I tell you a mystery: we will not all sleep, but we will all be changed—in a flash, in the twinkle of an eye.
1 Corinthians 15:51–52 (NIV)

The little prince told the pilot to leave the area of the well and come back tomorrow, which he did. When the pilot arrived the next day, it appeared that the little prince was having a conversation with someone. The pilot did not see or hear anyone but the little prince, who was talking about a particular spot or location he would be at when something occurred. The little prince then told the pilot that the conversation was about getting bitten by a snake and whether he would suffer from the poison in it. The pilot heard this and realized that the little prince was planning to die.

The little prince then came down from the wall he was sitting on, and the pilot saw the snake. The pilot, alarmed by the snake, tried to shoot and kill it with his sidepiece, but the snake made his escape.

When the pilot got to the little prince, he looked very sick. The pilot asked why the little prince had been talking to the snake. The pilot was concerned about the physical condition of the little prince and how weak he was becoming. Somehow, the little prince knew the pilot had fixed his engine. How could a little child learn this if he was only a little child?

The little prince disclosed that while he was on the wall with the snake, he knew that the pilot some distance away had already fixed his plane. How could this be? I'm reminded of when Jesus first encounters Nathanael: "Jesus saw Nathanael coming to him, and saith of him, Behold an Israelite indeed, in whom is no guile!" Nathanael was perplexed as to how Jesus knew him when they had never met before.

> Nathanael saith unto him, Whence knowest thou me? Jesus answered and said unto him, Before that Philip called thee, when thou wast under the fig tree, I saw thee.[158]

How could Jesus know that Philip went to find Nathanael before they ever met? Only by the knowledge of God. This is suggestive of the omniscient knowledge of God. Only God knows everything.[159] How else would the little prince know that the pilot had already fixed the plane's engine?

The pilot was coming to tell the little prince the good news! The only reply the little prince gave to the pilot was that he too was going home today. This was profound and yet upsetting to the pilot. The pilot wondered how the little prince would possibly get back to asteroid B-612.

The pilot sensed for the first time hidden under the beautiful laugh of the little prince was a sad outcome. The little prince now disclosed to the pilot that although it had only been eight days since they met, he had been on Earth for one year, and now his time on Earth was done. The pilot voiced his concern to the little prince about the snake and its dubious nature, but the little prince's mind was made up, and there was little the pilot could do to alter or change it. It was the code of how the little prince lived and dealt with his own sad life.

The pilot now remembered that the most important things cannot be seen with the eye. Is the pilot beginning to understand all that the

---

[158] John 1:47–49 KJV.
[159] 1 John 3:20 KJV.

little prince said to him about life, friendship, and even death? These are not tangible or physical but things of the heart, and the memories and love you experience with friends are the most important.

This coming separation from the little prince was more than the pilot could take. He once again wanted to hear the beautiful laugh of the little prince, and he feared he would never hear or see him again. The little prince was unchanged in his decision to leave Earth and go back to his planet, possibly asteroid B-612, by any means necessary.

The little prince tried to offer the pilot some comfort in this situation. The little prince said that when the pilot was flying his plane and looked up to the stars, he could think of him. His planet was so small that the pilot would not know which of the planets or stars the pilot saw at night would be that of the little prince. The little prince laughed and promised to laugh always, making the pilot happy when he looks to the stars. Then the little prince said some of the most beautiful words of comfort to ease the pain of the pilot:

> And when your sorrow is comforted (time soothes all sorrows) you will be content that you have known me. You will always be my friend. You will want to laugh with me.[160]

Memories of loved ones are so important to our creaturely existence. We all need to process separation and loss. Memories of those we love are good medicine for our soul. Remember, the most important things are those aspects of life you cannot see, the spiritual. The little prince knew the pain and suffering one experiences when a friend leaves. The little prince must have been thinking of that when he left his rose, or when he left his friend the fox and now the loving pilot.

The little prince tried to talk the pilot out of staying with him when he left this world to the next. Confused, the pilot was insistent that he would not leave the side of the little prince during this critical

---

[160] Saint–Exupéry, The Little Prince, p. 136

time. But during the night the little prince snuck off while the pilot was sleeping. When the pilot awoke to find him gone, he was able to locate him eventually, but it was too late.

The little prince tried to warn the pilot that the event would make him sad and cry because "I shall look as if I were suffering. I shall look as if I were dying. It is like that. Do not come to see that."[161]

The little prince told the pilot the reason he had to leave this body behind was that it was too heavy for the trip home. Then the little prince told the pilot something extraordinary, that when he transitioned back to his planet,

> You know, it will be very nice. I, too, shall look at the stars. All the stars will be wells with a rusty pulley. All the stars will pour out fresh water for me to drink.[162]

This fresh water does not appear to be the same type of water that they drank out of the well but much like the water pills that the merchant sold or the living water Jesus told the woman about. Why all these references to living water; the afterlife of eternity?

We have previously discussed that God has been likened to living water:

> My people have committed two sins:
> they have forsaken me,
> the spring of living water,
> and have dug their own cisterns,
> broken cisterns that cannot hold water.[163]

And Jesus said, "He who believes in me, as the scripture said, from his innermost being will flow rivers of living water."[164] It appears that the little prince may have understood these spiritual concepts

---

[161] Saint–Exupéry, The Little Prince, p. 136
[162] Saint–Exupéry, *The Little Prince*, p. 138.
[163] Jeremiah 2:13 NIV.
[164] John 7:38 NIV.

that were invisible to the eye. Living waters cannot be seen or drunk physically but only with spiritual understanding. Will the pilot come to understand this too?

So now the little prince was preparing to leave his physical body forever. The Bible teaches:

> Listen, I tell you a mystery: We will not all sleep, but we will all be changed—in a flash, in the twinkling of an eye.[165]

> Death has been swallowed up by victory. Where, O death, is your victory? Where, O death, is your sting?[166]

The little prince has told the pilot that he must go back to his rose; she needs his care and protection. In that instant, a flash, something, what we believe was the snake in the sand, bit the little prince on the ankle. The little prince then gently fell to the sand as though dead. The snake bit the little prince in the same area of the foot that was promised in Genesis 3:15:

> I will put anonymity between you and the woman and between your seed and her seed, he shall bruise you at the heel and you shall bruise him on the head.[167]

Did the little prince know the promises God had for him?

> Behold I have given you authority to tread on serpents and scorpions, and over all the power of the enemy, and nothing will injure you.[168]

The little prince had finalized his decision to leave earth and

---

[165] 1 Corinthians 15:51–52 NIV.
[166] 1 Corinthians 15:54–55 NIV.
[167] Genesis 3:15 NIV.
[168] Luke 10:19 NASB.

his bodily tent and go back to his planet, and the bite by the snake was the way. Would he now go back to the planet or be in the stars forevermore?

Wherever the little prince was going, he was sure of his destination.

For this seemingly children's book to have such an ending is extraordinary, and touches the most important aspects of life, death and the afterlife. The pilot is finally understanding these important elements of life.

Chapter 27

Going Home

But our citizenship is in heaven. And we eagerly await a Savior from thee, the Lord Jesus Christ.
Philippians 3:20 (NIV)

The pilot mentions that as he tells this story, it has been six years since his first encounter with the little prince. As I write, it has been six years that our son Christian's life was changed forevermore. The little prince has now ended his travels, much as our son Christian did, on the planet Earth. The little prince, too, was tired of his sad and tormented life, and left the body that brought him so much pain and suffering. He is now in his celestial home; maybe it's asteroid B-612, or maybe it's the stars or heaven. We don't know.

Many Christians believe what Jesus promised:

> Come to me, all of you who are weary and carry heavy burdens, and I will give you rest. Take my yoke upon you. Let me teach you, because I am humble and gentle at heart, and you will find rest for your souls. For my yoke is easy to bear and the burden I give him is light.[169]

---

[169] Matthew 11:28–30 NLT.

In all the little prince's travels and experiences, he appears to be searching for happiness, friendship, and the meaning of life. Now our sad little friend has found the most important thing he was searching for: peace and happiness, and the true meaning of life and the afterlife.

Rest, our little princes, in the comfort of the arms of the true pilot.

The Bible teaches us to be comforted in times of loss, suffering and sorrow: "Don't let your hearts be troubled. Trust in God and also trust in me."[170] Jesus also said,

> I am leaving you with gifts—peace of mind and heart.
> And the peace I give is a gift that the world cannot give. So do not be troubled or afraid.[171]

The gift that the little prince left the pilot is indelible in his life. Every time he looked to the stars, he knew he would be laughing although he would not know where the little prince was nor which star the laughter was coming from.

The pilot tells us the little prince's body could not be found after the bite from the snake, much as on the first Easter morning, when the women came to look for Jesus at the tomb but found the tomb empty. When they entered the tomb looking for the body of Jesus, all that remained was his grave clothes and nothing else. His body was not there. The angels then told the women that if they were seeking Jesus,

> He is not here, but is risen; remember how he spoke unto you when he was at Galilee saying that the Son of Man must be delivered into the hands of sinful men and be crucified and on the third day rise again.[172]

---

[170] John 14:1 NIV.
[171] John 14:27 NIV.
[172] Luke 24:6–7 KJV.

That the little prince's body was not there brought great comfort to the pilot, knowing that the little prince did in fact make the long journey home. The pilot was comforted by those things he remembered about the little prince: his inquisitive questioning, his contagious laughter, his beauty, his wisdom, and most of all his friendship.

But the pilot also worried from time to time what happened to his little friend. The pilot realized he had not drawn a strap for the sheep's muzzle so that the little prince could attach it to the sheep so the sheep would not eat his rose. The pilot, like us when we experience loss, vacillated from being comforted to being sad, but that is part of the grieving process and the loss of a friend or someone we loved.

Forevermore when the pilot would look to the stars and think of his little friend, he thought it was both "the loveliest and the saddest landscape in all the world."[173] The pilot's closing thought was something he remembered from the little prince when he said, "Then I am happy. And there is sweetness in the laughter of all the stars."[174] The most important things in life are things that cannot be seen with the eyes: "It is only with the heart that one can see rightly; what is essential is invisible to the eye."[175]

---

[173] Saint–Exupéry, *The Little Prince*, p. 144.
[174] Saint–Exupéry, *The Little Prince*, p. 189.
[175] Saint–Exupéry, *The Little Prince*, p. 112.

Afterword: Six Years On

Things get damaged, things get broken
I thought we'd manage but words left unspoken
Left us so brittle
There was so little left to give.

Depeche Mode, "Precious"

When I was preparing for the birth of my youngest son, I did not have a name for him. One night when I went to sleep I had a vivid dream. My dream was about the book *A Pilgrim's Progress*, written by John Bunyan in 1678, and its main character, Christian.

I saw the story come to life in my dreams. I saw a young boy carrying a large bundle of burdens strapped to his back. I saw the difficulty of the young man trying to navigate life carrying those heavy burdens. After a while, his travels ended and he reached his final destination: the celestial city.

Then it was revealed to me, I believe by the Holy Spirit, that like the character in the book and dream, "Your son too will have difficulties and burdens in life, but he will never depart from his faith." It was then revealed to me that I should call my son Christian after the character in *A Pilgrim's Progress*. With that, I woke up the next morning and knew the Lord had revealed to me the name of my son, which was to be Christian.

This book was the result of our own suffering and loss when our son Christian tragically died at the age of twenty after suffering catastrophic injuries in a motor vehicle accident. I did not believe that any good thing would come out of this tragedy, although we are promised that good will come out of life's difficult circumstances. Writing this book became an extension of healing. Through the healing process and dealing with the loss of our son, we came to understand that his life was parallel to that of the little prince. Each chapter from *The Little Prince* seemed to reflect the life and travails of our son Christian. That is how the book became so important in our life. It was uncanny how the book depicted how our son and the little prince lived, and how the little prince and our son left this life for the next—not too early, not too late, but at that precise moment in time.

Although we will miss Christian terribly, we now realize that much like the little prince, he is now free from his earthly tent where he suffered so many days of his life. Writing this book has given me a better understanding of life and how to appreciate each day as it comes, but maybe more importantly, of death and the process we will go through from life to death and unto the stars.

I have used *The Little Prince* to explain these theological concepts. My hope is that this work will bring peace, joy, and understanding that life on earth and our existence is only momentary—and eternity is forever and beyond.

I hope that this book has given you joy and hope for any loved one who, like the little prince, has departed this planet for the stars.

Milton Keynes UK
Ingram Content Group UK Ltd.
UKHW010853280324
440101UK00001B/242